I ESCAPE THROUGH YOU

Mike Arnold

You have to live through winter

to appreciate the summer in full.

1

A day wasted in Edinburgh Waverly. Hours faded away just watching the world pass by. I direct all frustrations towards the flickering delayed symbol on the overhead timetable. The cursed orange triangle patronises as it blinks. Six hours of travelling to arrive in this beautiful city, only to find it a slightly bitter variation of itself. Of course, cities can't be bitter.

It all stems from the unwelcome phone call from a particular website design company cancelling today's meeting. Everything cancelled. I guess that's just the culture these days.

Yes, I'd usually try hard to be the kind of guy you'd be at peace with such situations. Life sucks sometimes. Bear it and move on. Everything happens for a reason. It just wasn't meant to be. Yet today is different. Today it stings. Was it the meeting?

Maybe. Supposedly the start of my next chapter. Seemingly gone. Here I am, waiting on a blank page that feels as though it's never going to turn. It sounds cliche, but it was a chapter full of dreams. The early days of starting my own branding business. Finally on my feet. A brave new world.

It felt like progress, at least compared to the rut I had just climbed out. Now feeling more like a pipe dream that's never getting off the ground.

Sure, starting any business is never an easy journey, but it seems to become a challenge once you reach a stage where you must rely on other people. Especially when those other people are fancy website designers based in Edinburgh who claim they can take care of every aspect of your new website. But, ultimately, they leave you high and dry, stuck in a train station for the entirety of the day, waiting for a return train home that may never come. I guess disappointments like this happen within relationships of any kind. Business or pleasure.

It's not the guy's fault his baby came early, I remind myself. It's a joyous occasion! I take a deep breath. I've always loved Edinburgh. I've visited less than a handful of times, mainly when I was younger, but I've always had a soft spot for its character. So much old stone. It always seems to be raining too. Not that that's a bad thing.

It's more like the atmospheric rain you'd see in a movie scene. A son watches his mother leave. A bus passes a girl crying in a bus shelter, only to see the boy she loves standing on the other side of the road holding a drenched supermarket bouquet. I like that kind of rain. It's a shame I'm not in the mood to do some exploring. Turn this into a lovely day out. When was the last time I was here, maybe three or four years ago?

When I came to visit her? Damn, it's been that long?

The station feels like it's getting busier. A steady stream of human beings living out their lives. People pass locked in phone calls and queuing at the ticket machines, and that lingering smell, oh God, that beautiful smell. That is by far the worst part of today. Being an ex-smoker, days like today are always a trigger.

Today might possibly be the most nagging cigarette craving I think I've ever had. I've patrolled the front of the newsagents twice to kill time and managed to resist buying a pack, but I don't know how much longer I can hold off. Why is today getting under my skin? I need to take my mind off things and stop freaking out. Let's sit down and relax. Deep breaths.

I hesitate in the queue of the Starbucks just off platform five, stumbling my order to the barista. No clue as to what I want. My mind isn't with me. I can't wrap my head around anything. How can I be so in my head that I haven't even looked at the menu by the time I get to the front of the trickling queue?

"Can you just surprise me?" I ask the girl behind the

counter. Her expression remains precisely the same. I can't even be sure her mouth moved to speak when asking me what I wanted.

"No, sir. You've got to tell me what you want."

Say the first thing to come to mind. You don't care that much.

"Er, just a coffee then."

"What kind?"

"I don't care."

"Sir."

"Just normal. Whatever." I added 'please' as an afterthought. I mildly sigh at the fact we didn't go into the whole large/venti debate.

I tell her my name. She scribbles it carelessly on the side of a takeaway cup. I pay cash and get directed to wait at the end of the counter. I apologise for being strange under my breath. If she heard the comment, she ignored it. She moves on with her life, serving the couple behind me. I barely remember when it was legal to smoke indoors. I was young.

The only memory that retains clarity was sitting in a pizza restaurant with my parents. I can't have been older than five. For some reason, I think it may have been my birthday. There were balloons at the table, but had they been there the entire time, perhaps for a previous party?

The pizzas arrived at the table atop the trays balanced on the fingertips of a wide-eyed waitress who cheerfully advised the plates were still hot. In child-like awe, the dishes looked amazing, and I quickly lost myself in awe of what lay before me. Pure disbelief for what feast was about to unfold. So much so that her warning went a little over my head.

I don't recall the feeling itself, but I clearly screamed as the metal pan blistered my skin. After a lot of fuss from my mother and a couple of the nearby waiters, I sat quietly by the counter with my finger in a glass of cold water, carefully pushing the fresh blister against the surface of the bobbing ice cubes.

However, it wasn't ice that ceased the strange sensations, but rather the surreal sight of a man chain-smoking in the cubicle before me. Opposite him sat a beautiful girl. They must have been in their 30s, but I wouldn't have known then. Instead, my awe was replaced by his ability to blow smoke rings so perfectly, shooting them into the air to drift effortlessly in front of his companion. Sometimes she would blow them away into nothingness, filling the emptiness with a giggle. Other times she would try to grab one with her hand or push them gently in another direction. Sometimes she would let them float to her face and break over her skin. It was peaceful.

"Lucas. Black coffee."

A second Barista calls me over, snapping me out of my reverie. I nod my gratitude and weave my way to a random table through the crowd. Another thought comes to mind after stirring sugar from the thin paper sachets into my cup. My old daily sunrise pilgrimage.

That feeling of heading up to the rooftop of my London apartment to blow billows of cigarette smoke into the empty stillness of the waking world. Sometimes, I'd even manage a smoke ring myself if the air was still enough. I miss that. The serenity of those little half hours in the morning. Now I suffer cravings that lap at my nerve endings like waves against a cliffside, little by little eroding my willpower.

Maybe that's an ocean that will never dry up. Come on, global warming. Help me out. It is funny, though, how beautiful things can turn sour. And, I suppose, some things go the other way.

The cafè is humming with families and children, but I find myself unable to take my eyes off the teenagers sitting on the sofa a little way from me. If it wasn't so busy, I could have chosen to sit anywhere else, but they're right in my eye line. I can't help but stare as they kiss and whisper little nothings to each other. A random thought lodges itself in the forefront of my mind.

It would have been my and Megan's fifth anniversary today. Is it that random, or perhaps what's been unconsciously bothering me all day? That's got to be it. Surely. Think. The last time I was in Edinburgh was to see her. In my brain, some distance puzzle piece clicks into place. I pretend to read a copy of The Guardian someone disregarded on the table.

Maybe if I actually knew when the train was coming, I could go and see a movie or something instead. I haven't been to the cinema in a long time either. Newspapers will do for now. The Guardian is boring, as per. There are a few interesting ads with logos I would maybe have done a little differently had I my own branding business.

Of course, there's the usual political and world commentary stuff. A story on how the UK is ruining the education system, bankrupted and corrupted by those in power seems mildly interesting but too long for my current attention span. There's an opinion piece on transgender rights. Although not nearly enough, a bank manager in the US has been fined for fraud. A lot of low vibrations here today.

I've always found it strange how my feelings tend to be reflected in the world around me. Almost as though I'm manifesting them. Sorry rest of the world. I've never been big on the law of attraction. I've never made a vision board, for example, but some connections between inner thoughts and the outside world are uncanny. The vibe doth sometimes match. I do often wonder if I'm alone in this way of thinking.

When a sadness takes hold, a showcase of it seemingly appears around me. The world mirrors what we see on the inside. Streets filled with parents overflowing with nothing but stress and exhaustion, sometimes even a drop of regret, as they shout into their children's faces with little to no regard for the passers-by.

I see the same sadness when someone complains to

the manager when their favourite menu item is out, something that's wholly ruining their special day. Couples argue, and work deadlines are missed. It usually rains on those days. Not that nice kind of rain either.

I remind myself the opposite is true, and reality can work in reverse. It's never always as dark and depressing. There's always a balance. Those days where you wake up and your head feels good. Almost as though the universe has a little voice speaking up from inside you, telling you today will be a good day.

Everything can suddenly look so beautiful.

Couples and families pass each other in the street and resonate with a kind of relatability. A slight smile and a tip of a metaphorical hat between unknowing loved ones acknowledge the feelings that come with walking hand in hand with the person you're sharing this time of your life with.

The same love encompasses the adoring fussing of babies crying innocently in their pushchairs.

Young couples share desserts in cafés and throw pennies into arcade machines on beach-front piers, hoping for a teddy bear grand prize, a token treasure honouring the memory of that sunny afternoon for a lifetime. It takes me back to those days when love clouded teenage summers.

Being in love was innocent back then. Exciting. Passionate. A teen in love would do anything. Could do anything. Walk any distance, take any bus, find the money to buy any gift just to see their sweetheart smile. Nothing else could matter as much.

I sigh into my coffee and watch the steam rise. Glimmers of my smoky Monday mornings before work flash across my mind once again. My slightly forgotten urges for cigarettes return in their typical nagging fashion. I indulge them.

It's still better than staring ahead, trying to ignore the flirting teenagers for whom the wider world no longer existed. Lovers lost in their bubble. What happened to love being that easy? Is it actually possible to love someone in such a carefree way, with no inhibitions or stains from the past holding things back? I wonder if these two will experience the usual journey.

Love now. Break up later. Perhaps he cheats or gets bored, wanting to take a different path in life. Or the girl, who ignores her now-cold cup in favour of his attention, might wake up one morning and realise her life is heading in a new direction. She moves to Australia to work on an avocado farm or perhaps tries to find herself in Thailand.

With his pale Scottish complexion, her boyfriend would never last in a tropical country. They both become new people, stepping forward into forever-growing versions of themselves, and while they'll always have the sweet coffee shop moments they share in Edinburgh train station, one day, there will be a moment when they think of each other for the last time.

That hits something inside me. All relationships seem to end in their own strange ways for their own strange reasons. Sometimes as a quiet, sad ending that is more a fizzling, failing firework than a bang. Sometimes the entire box of rockets explodes at once. Then, once the dust has settled, those former lovers mourn until they don't.

They swipe right through sleepless nights, plagued by thoughts condemning them to be alone forever. They'll cover themselves in fresh clothes ordered last minute, attempting to hide the emotional scars from cut from new and passing partners.

The station loudspeakers declare the most recent travel updates overhead. I'm comforted to know that my train is now on route. I finally get to go home and leave this sodden city. The first steps in forgetting today are in motion. I feel determined. I'm going to find a new design company that works digitally and finally start snowballing my business dream. I'll make it happen.

A world and a metre away, the teenagers snap out of their bubble and fall back into reality to listen to the station speaker with me. He whispers something in her ear while scrunching the front of her t-shirt in his hand, his other arm wrapped around her back. Sitting on his lap, the girl giggles, pushing a lock of her hair back behind her ear.

He's slouched, hiding his height in the way teenagers do. Whatever he looks like to others, it feels nothing short of arrogant to me —almost a kingpin cliché. I'm conscious of my bitterness and swallow it. Even now, after seeking refuge in the café, passing the time with coffee and people watching, the glass station roof is making me feel like an ant trapped under a magnifying glass.

Maybe I'll simply spontaneously combust right here and now! That would be quite a way to go. Perhaps a panic attack from all the overthinking. In a moment, I've detached from reality and have instead found myself stuck experiencing my own time-lapse of the world beyond the doors of the coffee shop. A reality I'm no longer a part of. I can't help but stare ahead.

The faces of strangers pass in a blur of blended fleeting colours from the t-shirts and blouses, the rumbling of suitcase wheels, stifled coughs, and phone calls. Noise and colour becoming meaningless.

Everything bleeds together and becomes nothing. I let it wash over me and surrender to it all. I find myself relentlessly watching the lovers again, now ceasing their playfight of pouring sugar sachets over each other and instead smile into each other's eyes. They kiss. Something warms inside me. Some part of me, some deep-down part I haven't felt in a long time, sparks to life.

I miss her. I don't miss her. I miss something. But I don't want anything. I just want her to be okay. I hope she is. Wherever she is, I hope she was able to find happiness. I hope she was about to find her way. I feel guilt. Was it my fault? Did I make things worse? Was there anything I could have done better? I've surely thought about it. I can't look at the passing faces properly. I'm afraid I'll see her. And I'm afraid I won't.

I used to be unable to take my eyes off her, utterly breathless at the sight of her. That gut-punched feeling she always gave me. The sun shines bright in all my memories of her. At least, that's what I like to believe. It amazes me how such feelings can appear so suddenly out of nowhere and can fade just as quickly.

Thinking about it, do they ever really leave? Or do they just burrow deep? As much as I try to push the thoughts out of my mind, the memory of that year spent with her is looping somewhere in the back of my mind.

The year I spent loving and losing Megan with everything I had.

2

It was late spring and I was 24 years old when my life crossed paths with Megan's.

I lived in London in a small two-bedroom apartment rented with an old friend from school. Aaron. He was a decent guy. After we finished college, he was offered a well-paid job in a prominent investment firm. A little regretfully, I never really took the time to understand the ins and outs of what he did. Managing portfolios and creating spreadsheets, at a guess.

Whatever it was, his journey involved him starting at the bottom of the corporate ladder, and London is an expensive city for someone clinging onto that initial rung. He asked me to move in with him to help him get started. I agreed. After all, I didn't have anything better to do. No plans nor aspirations as such. I was lost in the woods, looking for my path. But I wanted to help Aaron.

He had always been good to me, and who knows what opportunities London had. Many, I imagined. And, for the first time, I had a space I could call my own.

I landed a job working in an upmarket Thai restaurant under the promise of a fast promotion that never came. It had been three long years of waiting tables since. It wasn't as though being a manager in a restaurant was a deeply held dream, so when it became clear it wasn't coming, I felt nothing. Perhaps a mild resentment, but nothing more.

It didn't take long for me to realise I was stuck in the typical dead-end job scenario, and I slowly decelerated, settling into living the bare minimum way.

The novelty of working in the Big City wore off rapidly. Work became an unrewarding means to an end. Paychecks fuelled nights drunk in the streets, parties in abandoned and sometimes not-so-abandoned warehouses, topped with fast food binges at weekends.

When money dried up, usually after the first of these weekends that month, video games became my escape from the dullness of everyday life. I've always been a fan of video games. Hours were spent exploring new worlds and fighting alongside some fantastic characters as a kid. We never had the latest consoles at home, but rather a Playstation One picked up from a boot sale once it was already obsolete, but I still loved it.

As I got older and my hardware improved, I was introduced to League. Yeah. Life fell into that rut. A simple five vs five game on the surface. Pick a character, learn the skills, and fight to defend your base while capturing your opponent's. But with over 180+ characters to play, each with their own abilities and personality, it was an easy game to play but hard to master.

It's fast-paced, exciting, and incredibly toxic. If an escape from reality is needed for a couple of hours, or you want to vent your bitterness towards the world out onto random strangers, then it's perfect in every way.

One unspecific evening, I sat down at the kitchen table, snacking on leftovers smuggled out from work while watching a video on how to play the League better with a single headphone in, my phone propped up on a cereal box. Work had been typical. Typical upmarket Londoners you'd typically expect in a typical fancy restaurant. Typical office workers drinking on company credit cards. Typical families demanding their typical big girl's birthday to be absolutely perfect. The usual. I got home exhausted. Aaron returned home around the same time.

"I can't believe it, dude," he said, waiting for the kettle to boil, prepping some ramen. He pinched a chicken ball from my plate in passing before continuing without prompt.

"So I went into the office, right? Gave the presentation and fuck me, it killed." He punched the air in triumph.

"Jason was the only other guy who made it. He could barely get his words out and stumped it completely. There was some other girl as well. Jane? Janine? I don't know. Anyway, they gave me the project man. How sick is that?"

"That's really cool, man. I'm really happy for you."

Enthusiasm escaped me. I was genuinely happy for Aaron and I tried. He worked hard. There was a specific inspiration in him and how he lived life. I just couldn't bring myself to show it. It's like receiving an invitation to an unforeseen wedding. Suddenly all this inner life evaluation begins from nowhere, forcing you to compare everything going on in your own life with that of everyone else's. Where am I compared to them? What milestones have I reached?

Fuck. I'm so far behind.

Everyone else is doing so well, and I'm still on the bench. Scratch that; I'm still in the changing rooms. Stuff like that. I've always thought this to be an evil kind of thinking.

"It's so good man. I'm so pumped to start. So many ideas. This is why we came to London! You know, it feels like things are finally starting to click into place."

"That's nice. I hope it goes well. You're definitely the right guy for the job."

"It's dope as fuck. How are things with you anyway? You look exhausted dude. Sorry. I don't mean to be rude."

"Yeah, I'm good man. Just work and stuff, you know?"

"I hear you man. No rest for the wicked!"

I high-fived Aaron, but he didn't seem to notice the half-heartedness in my wrist before leaving him in the kitchen as I went upstairs. His voice carried up from the hallway as he 'Hey'd' his girlfriend Amy on FaceTime before I closed them, along with the rest of the world, out through the symbolic shutting of my bedroom door behind me. I sat in the room's darkness for a little while, waiting for my computer to load.

Compared to the dull light of the city blurred behind my blinds, the light from my monitor flicking on was blinding. As had been my routine the last two years, I loaded up the League and waited in the queue to find a game, watching a YouTube video of kids meeting their favourite sporting heroes to pass the time. Then another. Billie Joel called a kid up on stage to let him play his guitar with the band.

Watching videos seemed to be another way to stop any thinking that may occur during the moments of silence that one inevitably finds themselves in throughout their life. It's a strange realisation to notice being sat in a room on your own. It's why I always wore headphones. This one was a pretty wholesome clip. The game began.

Megan and I were randomly paired on the same team. It's strange to think back to that night when she was nothing but a stranger on the Internet. A girl sitting behind a computer screen somewhere out in the world's middle. Just pixels. A series of moving electrical colours that impacted my life in ways I could never have imagined at that moment.

This is how big things happen, isn't it?

A new tiny stitch in the tapestry of our lives seems so inconsequential until later we see that it was the start of a whole new panel. This night was part of constructing the frame. The game itself played out incredibly well, and after a fantastic finish, we added each other to our friend's list and played a few more decent games back to back before going to bed, thinking nothing more of it. I'd played and added other people before.

Time passed. Me and Megan never spoke to begin with, only game-related talk congratulating each other on our plays or planning an attack, and even then we were only writing words on a screen. For several months, we occasionally played, but only if we happened to be online simultaneously. It wasn't until October that we decided to use the voice chat after playing together nearly every night of that week. And I have to say, I was surprised to hear a girl's voice on the other end of the line.

In a game dominated by toxic guys and hormonal teenagers and kids who take the game way too seriously and spout off aggressive, typically racial, slurs any time a mistake is made, it was a breath of fresh air to actually have fun playing. It was bliss.

Sure, we lost every round we played, but it didn't matter. I felt electric and actually enjoyed the game for what felt like the first time in forever. Even at that moment, I noticed I was actually having fun rather than using it as a crux or coping mechanism. Instead of destroying bases, we spent our time running around the virtual map, me chasing Megan's in-game character and then being chased by hers. We screamed at each other like kids playing kiss chase in a school playground.

While an entirely virtual experience, confined to the borders of a small screen, the time we spent together was freeing. Perhaps even liberating. But I didn't care. I didn't even think about it.

Whatever it was I felt, I knew I was hooked and couldn't help but smile through every second of it.

When I got up to fetch a drink, my bedroom's authentic darkness was slightly chilling compared to the warmth of being lost in space with Megan.

3

Towards the end of the week, we started to play for hours, and while we were blissfully unaware, early evening turned to early morning.

At some point we stopped playing and moved our conversation to bed, my laptop next to me emitting the only dim light in the room, although the sky had started to warm. I stared into the darkness of the ceiling, headphones on, completely lost in a conversation that spanned all the standard topics covered when getting to know someone new.

Simple questions with simple answers, maybe, and yet every syllable utterly captivating. Megan's on-screen avatar, a cartoon drawing of a sleeping ginger cat nestled into a cushion, glowed with a green ring around it with every word she spoke. Her voice sounded quiet, sprinkled with notes of shyness.

"I'm studying for a PhD. In law," she stuttered. "I'm half at the university and then work for a firm the rest of the time. It's kind of all the same thing jumbled together."

"Law. Eww. Sounds complicated. What year are you in?"

"Well, three years left but have done a year already. If I'm being honest, it's been a bit of a journey."

"How come? What do you do?"

"It's conservation law. It's crazy to think I'm actually doing it. When I was in school, I really wanted to work with animals, so then, when I was in Sixth Form, I signed up for this trip where a group of us went to Portugal to help put tags on dolphins to track them and where they go and where they have their young, and all that stuff. It was amazing."

I said nothing. I could listen to her talk all day.

"Anyway, that kind of sparked me really wanting to do something in conservation with animals and with the oceans, and found this PhD and thought this could be my way in. It's kind of confusing sometimes, at least it is to me, but it's all about the legal aspects of sustainable business. You've probably heard stuff about the planet going green. Or trying to, at least. I think it's cool anyway."

"What sort of stuff do you actually do in the course?"

"It's pretty random. Recently it's a lot of things like looking into the rules and regulations to do with sustainable fishing and not completely fishing out an entire species. Most businesses just think about the money all the time and not much else. Now there's rules and regulations they have to follow; they hire us to make sure they're doing it right."

"I'm imagining you're working for big food suppliers or oil rig companies, things like that?

"Well, the last year I've been working with companies who want to build hydroelectric dams in rivers and wind turbines in the ocean. You've probably seen them around without really noticing."

"No, I've noticed. My parents live about an hour from the coast, and there's a huge wind farm with 50 turbines or something like that built a few years back. Looks like a scene from the future to be honest."

"Yeah, those are the ones. There's a ton of legal stuff to do with animals being disrupted. There was a thing on the news a year ago about how the vibrations of turbines in the Midlands caused whales to wash up on the shore because they lost their way of migrating around the world."

"Yeah, I heard something about that."

"So what I'm doing, well, what our whole course is kinda working on, is trying to find the balance between protecting the oceans and marine life, and I guess the planet in general, and expanding the renewable energy industry in a healthy way. It's a fine balance that, as it turns out, is really hard to find."

"Wow. That all sounds amazing. It sounds like

you've really found something that you love as well. I can hear the passion in your voice."

"I am, and not really at the same time. Not loving it. I love the going-out-into-the-oceans bit and working with animals. We did another project tagging sea lions and it was so amazing to be so close to them. Most of the time it's just a lot of reading documents and researching. Lots of paperwork. When the energy companies come in, I make a lot of the tea."

"So, you basically wait on people too? Seems like we have a lot in common."

"You're funny."

"Have you thought about leaving the research-y bit and just doing the field stuff like tagging animals and that? I don't know how it works, but there might be a way."

"I don't know. My parents were kind-of pushy with wanting me to do a PhD and be the first one in the family to get a university education. I didn't really know what I wanted to do properly after Sixth Form, so I just kind of went for it. I actually only joined because my friend Daisy was doing it, and she only enrolled because a guy she liked was doing it. Anyway, that was years ago, and Daisy moved away last year, so yeah. That happened. There may or may not have been a guy I liked who was also doing it, but I won't get into that now."

The last sentence slipped past me, and I let it. The sound of something stuck in her throat gave something away.

"I'm not judging. Each to their own. What did you want to do when you were younger? Did you always want a job where you saved the world?"

"I never really had a dream job. But I loved spending time outside when I was small, so I knew I always wanted to do something outdoorsy. We had horses at home, and I'd always ride and hang out with them after school. Sometimes in the summer, I slept in the stables with them. I did want to be a vet at one point, but I can't stand the sight of blood. Makes me want to pass out."

"I think it's nice like that. Being close to animals, I mean. Not the passing out to blood bit. I remember walking through the city the other week and noticing how all these different species of birds and animals, like squirrels and birds and deer if you go to Richmond Park, all get on with each other so well. Then as soon as a person walks by, they all run away. But they don't do it to each other. Sad it's hard-wired into them to run away from humans."

"Yeah, instinct. I love putting the time in though. We had loads of pets at home when I was small. I mean a lot, like three dogs and four cats kind of a lot."

"Don't forget the fish and guinea pigs."

"And how did you know that?"

"Anyone who says they had many pets definitely had fish and guinea pigs. Let me guess. One fish ate the other at some point?" Megan laughed and agreed.

"I don't know if I would like birds as a pet though. My dad's friend had this hawk he kept in his garden. It was a pretty mean looking thing. I also went to a bird of prey centre once, and you know they do the displays and fly the birds around, and the people tell you all about them? I think they were doing a display with a harrier hawk, and it chased me around the arena. I think I was five, so obviously I thought I would die," she said, laughing.

When she laughed, I saw stars.

Like someone had climbed up and stuck those glow in the dark constellations onto my grubby, peeling apartment ceiling.

"Aww, it just wanted to be friends with you!"

Talking with Megan was effortless.

Speaking with her reminded me of what it was like to date during school when everything felt innocent, not yet made murky by the push and pull of sex. Tides of desire. We spent hours that night sharing everything we could.

Not wasting a second. Our favourite songs. Favourite foods.

Back then, she was reading Stephen King. She adored all the dark psychological twists and turns of the story, but her favourites included classics like Hemingway and Scott Fitzgerald.

I'd never been a fan of them myself since they always seemed far too difficult to read. The language was strange. She loved them and told me how she could spend days losing herself in those written worlds. Her love for them made me want to love them too. Yet, despite being something she loved, she only read rarely. Only when she could find the motivation to read, which in itself wasn't often. When she did, she would finish an entire book in a day or two.

Megan shared her travel experiences, as did I. She had explored a lot of Europe the summer between finishing Sixth Form and starting university. She spoke bad French and only had a sweet tooth for jam doughnuts. The rest of her diet was pretty much savoury foods only.

She dove into the tales of how she'd slept under the stars, swam in lakes, and shared the only time she's ever been drunk that resulted in her passing out in a back alley in Barcelona.

My favourites from her collection were the ones of her sleeping out in the stables during her summer months she spent at her parent's house in the south of France.

I told her about the time I got food poisoning in a hostel in Naples, and it was so hot I ended up sleeping out on the roof, not realising the door locked automatically. I'd forgotten how much vomiting was involved. Megan didn't mind - instead laughing so much the story took twice as long as usual to tell.

We arrived sleepily and unknowingly at half four in the morning, the curtains glowing with morning light once more.

Our voices grew softer and softer until we exchanged nothing more than faint mumbles and then nothing. I lay in bed, exhausted by talk, basking in the silence. Rocking on the verge of unconsciousness myself, it was a comforting feeling knowing Megan was probably silently asleep just there on the other side of the screen.

I look back and think it may have been a creepy thing to do - to stay up and listen to a somewhat-complete stranger sleeping, but it didn't feel like a problem. It actually felt quite right.

Megan's alarm screamed distortedly through my laptop speakers a few hours later. We quickly exchanged good mornings and wished each other a pleasant day. We then repeated it all over again the next night.

We hadn't planned on it, but the foundation-less hope of repeating the joys of the night before made me so excited to finish work and return home. Each second of that day crawled. Work dragged. I craved spending more time with Megan so profoundly that, come the end of my shift that evening, I convinced my manager to let me lock up alone to save him the trouble of staying himself.

Don't worry, I've got your back, I said to him. I then proceeded to close everything down and left ten minutes early. The walk home felt like I was walking home on one of those moving floors at airports, only it was in the wrong direction.

I burst in the door to the apartment, nodded to Aaron and Amy cuddling on the sofa in the lounge, switched on my computer, and sure enough, there was the little green dot confirming that she was online.

I sighed with relief and waited in the game menu for her to finish her current match, but I kept myself from clicking on her to see if she would message me first. I didn't want to seem too eager after all. Plus, I wanted to know she had enjoyed last night as I had. Clearly her messaging first would be a sign of that. She was all I'd thought about all day, and I'm sure she'd been in my dream in some form or another. Could she possibly have been imagining me all day, too?

Picturing my stupid avatar and replaying our conversation while she looked through legal regulations for wind turbines and created presentations for energy companies or whatever she was filling her day with. I waited while scrolling on my phone until a message notification popped as soon as she was out of her game.

"Hey you." she wrote.

Off we went.

We spun down the digital rabbit hole into our own little fantasy world. I don't know what I would have done if she never messaged me first. I can only guess I would have caved and messaged anyway, no matter how desperate that may have made me seem. The same happened the following night and the next, until our spontaneous evenings became our routine.

A week passed before we swapped phone numbers, and not long after, we spoke nearly every single hour of every single day, be it through game chats, text, and video calls.

The first time we video called, and I saw her face for the first time, I didn't even know what to say. She was just as beautiful as I had imagined. I liked Megan a lot. She was a free spirit. An animal lover.

She was kind, caring and had big dreams of living on a farm in the mountains, somewhere like the north of Spain, or on the borderline of a forest. It's there she would start her own family.

She was also fun and daring, though some might call her slightly reckless, and enjoyed taking spontaneous trips abroad or camping in random fields more than anything. She didn't have much of an opinion on typical life stuff, like the mainstream political stuff on the news, and had no interest in pop culture, but that suited me fine. She just did her best to get the most out of education and tried to capture as much happiness as she could throughout each and every moment.

In fact, Megan often described the best kind of day as a day when she simply smiled. Even if she only smiled once.

Maybe I should have noticed that this smiling philosophy of hers had a dark side.

How often did a day pass when she didn't smile at all?

4

It hadn't been a month before we decided to meet in person.

Megan had planned to visit London for a renewable energy conference, Financing Wind Europe, of which her university supervisor stated that attendance was mandatory. Yet it was a conference she had absolutely no interest for.

"I think the university just suckers people in on their first year by offering these amazing trips and opportunities, and then once you've signed up, you just have to sit in an office all day and do their paperwork," she said one night, a week before the event was due.

Her voice confessed her frustration and tiredness.

"Well, I think it's more what you can get out of it. Once you've finished your course and got your PhD, you'll be able to go and work on conservation projects without much problem, surely? Then you can be hand's on with it."

"I doubt that Lucas. I've fucked up. I haven't done animal studies or biological sciences. I've chosen law. I think I'm destined to stay behind a desk and computer screen for the rest of my life."

"There's always time to change, Megan. You don't have to stick with your course, you know? You do have the option to leave if you really don't like it. How long have you got on it now?"

"Like two years."

"Imagine if you quit and started working on biological sciences, or even working on volunteer projects. Maybe you'd enjoy that more."

"It's not that easy Lucas."

"Why not?"

"I'm doing my PhD. I have to. My parents would be so unhappy and disappointed if I quit. I was taught never to quit anything."

"Well, that's a good mentality. I suppose. Unless you're talking about smoking. Finish what you started, that kind of thing. But if it's stressing you out so much, what's the point in staying?"

"Lucas. Just don't. I'm doing the PhD."

"I know, I know. I'm just saying you always have a choice."

"I think I'm just going to go for one day. Probably the first. I can sign in, show my face, and get out."

Our computers beeped as a new game began.

"Well, if you're doing your whole PhD, maybe you should go for the whole conference. I mean, the whole point is to learn something." I teased playfully.

"Lucas, you don't know how boring those things can be. It's just a load of older people talking about cost-investment risk and public relations. And you're forced to talk to other people. They ask you questions and ask for opinions I don't have." She was appealing to the introvert inside me. I didn't blame her. I wouldn't want to go either.

"Yuck. Still though."

"Nah. I've done enough of these to know it's not worth going. Besides, I have a report deadline that's stressing me out. I'd rather stay in and get that done."

"When's it in for?"

"About a month, but I've only done the first draft and haven't referenced anything. Then I have two company cases to work through with Sam. I just don't know what to do." Megan grunted with frustration and sighed forcefully. The game had loaded, and we set off to fight the pixel enemies.

"It's okay. There's no need to stress. You'll find a way to get it all done."

"Hmm."

"Anyway, like you said, how about you go for the first day, then go back home, and you'll have two days just appeared out of thin air to get ahead. I'm sure you could do a lot with two days?"

"Yeah. That's what I'm doing to do. I'm going to travel down the day before anyway. You know I said the conference is in London, right?"

"You did say something about that, yeah."

"Well, I was thinking, maybe, you'd want to meet up? If you wanted to, of course."

"Like come to the conference with you?"

"No. Don't worry, I wouldn't betray you like that. It would be torture, and they'd never let you in without a pass. But the university pays for the hotel I'm staying in? You could come stay with me the night before?"

I was so excited at the idea I could hardly contain myself. So excited I felt sick.

"Yes, that sounds amazing."

Tone it down Lucas.

"I mean, yeah. I think that'll be nice." Nice. So verbose.

"Well, I still need to confirm everything and book my place. Just the first day. Okay. I guess I'll see you then?"

"Sounds like a plan."

Megan confirmed her place at the conference and booked the hotel and train ticket the next day. The process was started and over in less than thirty minutes. We were meeting for the first time, and it felt as though my entire world was on fire.

During our calls from that day on, I'd kept my cool. I was calm and collected. However, once we hung up or had a momentary lapse in our daily texts, basically any moment I was left alone with just my thoughts, I let them race freely to create all the beautiful possibilities of what meeting up could be.

Was it going to be love at first sight? Would we fall into each other's arms? Would we kiss the moment we met? Would we hold hands through the station? Was this going to be the beginning of the rest of my life? How did Megan feel and think about it all?

There was clearly a connection between us, but I'd be lying if I denied there was a shadow feeling underneath it all. Was it nervousness or a deeper worry? A little fear maybe? Anxiety? Were we going to be the same people in person as we were online and on the phone? What if we weren't? I forced myself to ask instead what if we were. How amazing would that be?

It was hard to know whether to be more excited or afraid. After the booking was confirmed, the build-up over the first few days was nothing short of intense. I felt like we knew each other so well, despite only knowing each other for such a short time, but the connection was there.

Talking to Megan, hanging out with her, and feeling all teenager-esqe feelings blossom had been effortless. It had already got to the point where we quite possibly knew each other more intimately than anyone else on the planet did. Yet, suddenly and undeniably, our conversations developed a sober note.

"What if we don't feel the same in person? What if you're different?" she asked one night as we lay in bed,

300 miles apart. My phone propped upright against a stack of half-read books that now lived on my bedside table for that sole purpose.

"I don't think that's going to be a problem because I'm not a different person. I'm me. You're you. It's going to be fine," I said, reassuring myself just as much as her.

"But we don't know each other's, er, what's the word? Mannerisms? Like our habits or anything like that? What about if you pick your nose and eat it?"

"What if I do?"

"I don't know. I might not like it. I only know you through a screen. We could be so different in real life. What if you think I'm different? What if you don't like me? I know I'm just nervous, but..." She screamed and buried her face into her pillow.

"It's okay. I'm nervous too. I'm sure it will be fine when we're together. Probably just best not to think about it until we get there! Maybe try and be excited?"

"It's just so much pressure."

"Just relax. Let's have fun with it. How does that sound?"

"I know. I just get stressed out easily."

"I can tell," I teased, "It's fine. Anyway, what do you mean you might not like it if I picked my nose? You wouldn't be grossed out by it?"

"I don't know."

"Wait, hold on. Do you pick your nose and eat it?"

"Maybe. Sometimes."

"Ewww, that's gross Megan."

"Don't you?" She giggled.

"I mean sometimes. Only sometimes though."

"Ewww, that's gross," she teased back, mimicking my voice. We both laughed. I saw stars. I felt giddy.

"See, everything's going to be fine, no matter who we are in person. I promise."

Megan sighed. "I'm just really nervous Lucas."

"Me too, but hey, whatever happens, happens. That's just how life goes."

"Yeah, I know", she sighed, and I watched her cosy down under her duvet. "I just really like how things are now. I don't know if I can deal with that change. What if we don't connect, and it ruins this?"

"Megan. Ssh. Stop worrying. It's going to be fine."

"Sorry." She was right in the sense that everything felt so right how it was now. Now made me happy. Why risk and potentially throw away everything we had? It could have been so easy to break the illusion we had of each other. With Megan, I had found my escape. The question I kept asking myself was whether I was prepared to lose it all?

My mind kept travelling to the exact moment we would meet, and our connection would be tested for the first time. What would we talk about? How would our voices sound in real life? Would it be like everything I could imagine? Would it be completely different?

Would everything we've already built fall apart like

the pulling of a loose thread at the seams of a favourite worn jumper?

5

Our trains arrived at King's Cross station within an hour of one another.

I arrived first, since I only lived on the other side of the city, but I planned to get there early so she wouldn't be waiting for me. I zig-zagged my way up from the underground to sit outside the station on the large concrete blocks the city calls a bench, of some kind. A beggar pinned me to my seat to ask for money, weed, or both.

For some surreal reason, I pretended to be foreign speaking broken English to try and put him off speaking with me.

While trying to end the conversation as soon as possible, I misread Megan's text and her platform number, meaning I had to roam around to track it down. We shared our locations from our phones, and I found myself staring at everyone's passing face trying to figure out who I was actually looking for. I only had Megan's pixelated on-screen face to go by. How could I be sure that was what she looked like?

There's a saying, that time stands still for key moments of life. I don't know the actual saying, but it's written with words to that effect. I never understood what that saying meant until that moment. The moment that I first laid eyes on her.

I can't remember ever feeling so present.

6

There she was.

Leaning against a large stone pillar, the blur of people passed by.

The crested sea of hats and hair stood her out like a beacon in the night. A sudden clarity like the twisting of a camera lens. Life felt cinematic. I felt her. She scanned the faces of the crowd, looking for a face she recognised. Looking for me. After several lonely years in London, it was a feeling I wasn't used to, but damn, was it welcomed.

To see someone both nervous and excited to meet me. Quite unbelievable.

I saw her. The real her. Standing out like a bonfire on a dark autumn night. Warm. Inviting. Potentially scary. Daring me to come closer. Inexplicably yet so naturally drawing me in. Pure instinct made me move toward her. Her chocolate hair even resembled flames flicking out the sides of her starlight-grey bobble hat.

I started to pick my way through the crowd, bumping against the shoulders of silent strangers. From our early phone conversations, I knew that Megan nearly always wore the same clothes, despite owning wardrobes full of outfits. Usually, she'd choose the same green pastel woollen jumper, of which she had both a light and dark version.

As I stepped closer, there were the complimentary blue denim jeans with faded crease marks at the top, coupled with the frayed red canvas belt she had worn every day for as long as she could remember. After years of service, the ends of the belt that wove through the loops on her waistline were frayed along their entire edges from being pulled tight countless times.

Barely through the passing gaps of the crowd, like my own personal zoetrope, I made out the same worn hiking boots she wore through city streets and up mountainsides alike. I slowed my walk down on approach to watch her for the moment. Not at all because I was nervous. Her wonderful face was now clear in the sunbeams that glistened through the station's glass-domed roof. She held the scuff of her jumper sleeve, today the dark one, in a small ball in her fist and chewed a loose thread while her eyes darted across the crowds in front of her, her other hand tucked under her elbow. She looked nervous.

My stomach tightened. Please, Lucas. Don't mess

this up, I begged myself. Don't fall over. Don't say anything stupid. The thought was quickly replaced with another, telling me to grab her shoulders and make her jump. That could have been funny, maybe slightly scary, but Megan had already turned in my direction before I had the chance to act on it.

We made eye contact.

I was there. She was here.

There was no kiss. I didn't even lean in to try. I couldn't. Kissing felt a long, long way away. We hugged awkwardly. A nervous laugh. I was bumped from behind by a passing elderly silver-haired woman with a suitcase who grunted at me. I stumbled slightly into Megan. We thunked into the stone station column together. Nervous laughter.

"Well hey there. Fancy seeing you here."

"Didn't expect you here so soon?"

"How was the train?"

Should I hold her hand? No Lucas. Too soon. Chill.

"It was okay." She hesitated after she answered, then remained silent. I sighed at my awkwardness.

"Sorry. I suddenly feel really nervous. I was confident on the way over, I swear."

Our small laughs were muffled by overhead station announcements blaring from the speaker installed directly above us. I forced an awkward smile.

"Shall we?" I held my hand out, showing her the way. We set off towards the exit, our feet in step but apparently little else.

As we walked, the noise from the station blurred around us; she continued to chew the cuff of her jumper, finishing off the piece of loose thread until it was cut clean off. She then shoved her hands quickly under opposite armpits once she realised I was watching her.

"Are you nervous?" I asked.

"Yeah, a bit." She meekly looked up at me. "Okay, a lot."

"I tried eating on the train, but the thought of digesting food made me want to throw up. There was a baby opposite as well, so not sure that would have gone down too well if I had just spewed everywhere."

"Eww. I'm the same. I actually gagged a bit thinking about it, and the man opposite was staring at me. I'm pretty sure I actually threw up in my mouth. I dread that it smelled." Awkward laughing. Perhaps an undertone of authenticity.

Okay, a fraction of our video call comfort started to colour the conversation as we reached the station's exit and made our way into the high street.

"One second," Megan said, pulling out her phone to open the maps app. What I assumed to be the hotel's postcode was already pasted into the search bar.

She hit Go before spinning around on the spot several times to make sure we were pointing in the right direction, which I couldn't help but laugh at.

"What?"

"Nothing. Just funny watching you spin."

"Sorry. I suck at directing."

We set off onto Euston Road. The London traffic was typically unforgiving. Any chances to cross were well hidden between the speeding white vans and classic black taxis. Feeling slightly less nervous, the world seemed to become less blurred. The city was already plastered with Christmas decor displayed in surrounding shop windows and along both sides of the street, despite only being October.

Reels of rainbow gemstone lights hung from lamp posts, strung from one to another in a rudimentary fashion. A Christmas tree stood in the clear space outside the main terminal building. Holly wreaths stuck to bus stop corners. It all seemed to get earlier every year.

While I'd usually wait for the chance to cross the crazy roads of central London, Megan abruptly darted across to the other side of Euston Road, seemingly without looking for a gap in the traffic.

A red car slammed on the brakes and blew its horn explosively, an aggressive gesture she ignored. Even from the pavement, I could see her keeping her head down and watching her phone. I was stunned. She didn't even seem to notice. Not even a slight flinch.

I hopped across the road in front of the same car, waving sheepishly and giving the driver a slight nod. The driver returned exaggerated disbelief, hand gestures and all. I jogged briefly to catch up.

"Wow. You're really eager to get to the hotel, aren't

you?"

"Hmm, what do you mean?" She hadn't noticed. Fair enough.

"You okay with the map?" I asked. "I'm not too bad with directions. "

"It's okay," she said, spinning the phone around again on her palm. "It's good for me to figure it out. I seem to have a talent for getting lost, and I'm so bad at finding my way again." We set off down a quieter side street.

The roaring of the traffic seemed to fade out behind us quickly.

"I went to Girl Guides when I was a kid, and we did orienteering some weekends around a National Trust park. It was massive, but I always got lost. Everyone would always get back at least half an hour before me, so they started sending a supervisor to escort me around. It wasn't that much fun after that, so I quit."

We laughed. Still seeing stars as I heard it.

"Sorry," she added, "I'm babbling. I speak like this when I'm nervous."

"No, no. You're fine. Less awkward than not talking at all." I glanced at Megan every couple of seconds. She never took her eyes off her phone. Just take it slow Lucas. Nothing to worry about. It's just like talking on the phone. No pressure.

"So, when was the last time you were in London?" I asked.

"About a year or so ago."

"Oh yeah? Special occasion?"

"Yeah, the Winter Wonderland fair thing."

"Who did you go with?"

"A few friends, but I hated it. It's so expensive and so busy."

"Yeah, I haven't been to the Christmas stuff here in years. Actually, I don't think I've been while living here. I think I went more times when I lived near Norwich and got the train down with friends."

"Do you like living here?"

"Not really. I've always lived in the countryside with fields and trees. Never so much concrete. There was a big country park near where I grew up, with an amazing forest. I miss it all a lot." I really did.

"What about you?"

"Yeah, I prefer the countryside to cities as well. Too much concrete here."

"London's so dirty as well," I said. A line of overflowing brown, black and green bins and white rubbish bags with grey liquid visibly pooling out the bottom of them were piled high against the low stone-brick wall next to us.

"Yeah. It's gross. Look at the pavement. It's all chewing gum, cigarettes, and spit." Megan made a 'blah' sound and stuck her tongue out. "And the air tastes funny. I think my boogies are going black."

"Don't you mean boogers? But yeah, make sure you don't eat them."

"I would never." A wry smile.

"I don't know, it's a pretty weird city. I used to come with my parents like one weekend a year when I was a kid, but it was kinda disappointing. Have you seen the stuff like the Millennium Dome and Big Ben? When you see them in real life, don't you think they're so disappointingly small? The Eiffel Tower is massive."

"I don't know. I've never been, but I see what you're saying. Big Ben is more like a Little Bit Taller than Average Ben."

"Hmm. Just feels a bit pants."

"Yeah, I know what you mean. I just don't really like London. I think I have bad associations here though."

"How come?"

"Last time I came here was for a hen night with some friends from school. Must have been four years ago? Something like that. Daisy was there. It was so horrible." I recalled Megan telling me she didn't drink because it triggered panic attacks.

"Everyone was so drunk. We tried to get into four clubs and couldn't because my friend Tamsin, she was the one getting married, was so drunk. Couldn't even walk. We tried to get a taxi, and the maid of honour was mugged while trying to find her card."

"Damn, that's really unlucky. Were you secretly okay with it? I know you said you hated nightclubs. Sorry she got mugged as well. That really sucks."

"Hmm. Perhaps a lesser of two evils in that situation," she shrugged. "Wait, why are you saying sorry? Was it you?"

"Hmm, maybe." I winked, "Maybe I'm back for seconds. Just kidding. But it is a pretty dark city. There are always horror stories of gangs and things like that. Someone I used to work with was stabbed, but I think he was into drugs and that sort of thing." I knew he was, but I didn't want to admit it. "Shame it all happened on her hen night. What did she say afterwards?"

"Nothing really. They didn't really remember. I put them all to bed when we managed to get back to the hotel. Finally. Even getting there was terrifying. We got a lift in some random guy's sports car. I kept thinking he could take us anywhere and was probably kidnapping us. What would we be able to do about it? We did actually get to the hotel in the end. Kind of surprising. We woke up a few hours later and went home. They were all talking on the train about how amazing the night was."

"Huh. You're not going to do something like that for your hen night then?" "My hen night?" "I mean, are you going to have a big piss up in the city before you get married?"

Megan twisted her mouth to the right in thought.

"Maybe, but I'd rather do something quiet. Maybe stay near a beach or something and just have fun. Play board games with some friends in the evening. That sort of thing. Nothing crazy or intense. I like chill." Megan was silent for a while. Thinking about her beach plans and board games, I suppose. Did she want to sunbathe and drink from pineapples, or was she a pebbled shore and windy walks girl? I was about to dig deeper when she looked over at me. "What about you?"

"Yeah, I'm going to have the biggest hen night you've ever seen!" Weird images of me in a wedding dress, my male friends as bridesmaids, punching the air to techno music in a darkened nightclub flashed across my mind. I laughed at the idea and glanced at Megan pushing her hair behind her ear. She did that a lot, with little thought. It would be an image I would often return to, even years later. She still couldn't look directly at me, but even much later on, months after meeting for the first time, I would glance at her and find her in her own world, looking at something far away and pushing her hair back like that. Although, it was only ever in hindsight I only ever put together that it was a tell of hers. A nervous habit.

"I don't know though. Depends if I ever get married. It's a long way off yet." I said. My nerves were starting to really fade away. I could feel my true self coming up to the forefront of my being. I smiled to myself as an opportunity to tease Megan came to mind.

"Why don't you think you'll get married?"

"Well, I'm only 18, aren't I? I've got at least another ten years to think about that. Something like that," I said, stifling a laugh. Megan shot a glance in my direction so quickly and abruptly that her foot slipped down the curb's edge, and she stumbled out onto the road, narrowly avoiding a car passing us.

"Wait, what?" She spat, repositioning herself back onto the pavement.

"Yeah," I lied, trying so hard to stifle my laugh I had to turn to look down the passing street next to us. "You knew that, right?" Megan looked flustered but said nothing. It was nearly dark, and the car lights and street lights were flickering on around us, the shops illuminating our faces as we passed their windows.

I kept stealing glances at Megan, whose face was lit golden store after store. We crossed another junction as Megan kept her eyes down on her phone still, not daring to look at me. I allowed another few awkward seconds to pass.

"Relax. I'm just kidding" I finally laughed. Megan said nothing, then laughed and put her hand over her heart.

"Oh my god. You can't do that. I'm too gullible!" She breathed a noticeable sigh of relief. Her shoulders dropped.

Then a couple of moments passed before she asked, "Wait, so how old actually are you?"

"I'm 24. Don't you remember me telling you?"

"Well, yes, but. How do I know you're not lying?"
"You think I lie about my age to get older girls to meet up with me, and then I tell them my actual age before..." I trailed off. I didn't want to imply I thought there was a specific, intimate reason we were meeting

up. That's not what I wanted this to be. I didn't want Megan to feel like I did want it to be like... Oh no.

I condemned myself for even taking the conversation to that place at all. Almost instantaneously, it punished me for talking about marriage and weddings. Who talks about those things when they've just met someone? "Before we what?" she inquired, but she couldn't hide the smile on her face. Thank God.

"Before I get to know them on a deeper, more personal level." I teased back.

"Hmm. I bet." She was smirking.

"Just so we're clear. I'm 24. How old are you?"

"Well, wouldn't you like to know?" she teased back.

"Well, you're not underage, are you?"

"You know I'm 23, but I get ID'd for everything. I look like I'm 15, don't you agree?" Megan did have a babyface, but she was in university, so she couldn't be much younger than I was. All of a sudden, there was a slight shift in the atmosphere. A strange tension.

We'd found ourselves in this weird place where we knew we were joking, but we were also beginning to question if what we knew about each other was true. Had I been cat-fished? Did Megan worry she had been cat-fished?

"Okay, enough enough enough. Just show me your driving license to be sure," she insisted, holding out her hand.

"Wait, you don't believe me?"

"Well, I don't know now." She used her sleeve to hide the fact she was blushing. I pulled my driving license out of my wallet and handed it to her. She sighed in relief as her phone pinged.

We had reached the entrance to the hotel.

7

The Grand Mason stood before us.

Megan shook her head, smiling, clearly embarrassed she'd fallen for such a simple tease.

"And yours?" I asked. She handed it over from her purse. Everything checked out.

"So, if I was 18, what would that have meant?" I asked, climbing the concrete steps into the foyer. In case you somehow missed the massive glass doors of the entrance, there was a large red arrow stuck to the floor pointing in that direction. I held one of the large doors open for her to pass through but remained holding it for a further three families and a couple who squeezed through, heading in the opposite direction. I said thank you several times, despite being the one holding the door. Most of them muttered it back, mainly keeping their eyes on the floor they trod.

Megan was waiting on the other side by a white stand topped with a vase of large pink flowers. The foyer was so incredibly bright, especially having just come from the world of darkness of the night outside. Everything was clinically white.

"I don't know. Probably would have just run away," Megan continued from where we left off as I reached her.

"That's good to know." We made our way through the foyer to the front desk. With my eyes now adjusted, the hotel appeared surprisingly nice. The restaurant's glass walls that spanned one side of the reception seemed ultra-modern, as were the white tiled floors set with a wave pattern grooved into them, like the abstract patterns usually found in marble surfaces.

There were countless lights, a high ceiling, and fancy tables positioned around the outside of the foyer, each mounted with an iPad for checking in. It was designed, at a guess, for business people and travellers with a modest budget. It dawned on me that I hadn't stayed in a hotel for a long time.

Megan signed in with her debit card, and we took the lift to the fourth floor, sharing it with a typical German tourist-looking couple who smelt like Christmas market food. Sausages with caramelised onions. In true hotel fashion, the opening lift doors revealed a long red-carpeted hallway that stretched out before us, enclosed by dozens of rooms.

A couple of doors from the lift, a cleaner took a

handful of wrapped miniature soaps out from her supply trolley and disappeared into one of the open rooms. We passed her as she came back out, but she didn't so much as give us a second glance. We found the room, No. 412, fiddled the card into the slot above the door handle, and locked it behind us.

Instantly, I was hit by that classic hotel smell. A strange mix of fabric softener, scented bleach, and recycled air. The hotel's illusion of hygiene. After dropping her bags on the small sofa underneath the television, Megan lay straight down on the bed.

I was surprised a university would have covered the cost of such a nice-looking room. Perhaps I assumed they might have restricted students to a simple, budget-friendly option. Then again, I'd never been to university, so that I wouldn't know any difference. Perhaps they invested in their students more than I imagined.

I explored the room, the unwritten rule of checking in, pulling out drawers to see if there was anything interesting hidden within them, flicking switches here and there to see what happened.

Everything seemed standard. A hairdryer and an empty minibar aside from the two cooled bottles of white label water. There were little plastic pots of milk, sugar sachets, and a pot of little wooden stirring sticks on the desk underneath the TV, but no kettle or mugs.

The most exciting feature was an iPad on the bedside table resting on a pedestal on a fancy-looking wireless charging stand. A quick swipe revealed apps for controlling the TV and changing the colours of the lights in both the bedroom and the attached bathroom. I swiped my finger over the colour wheel and watched the light in the room change with my gestures from green to blue to red. Megan watched with child-like wonder on her face.

"Here." I passed the iPad over to her, and she was instantly captivated by the idea of the jellyfish-hued lights. She rubbed her finger around the wheel, mesmerised. She then blinked, surprised, and apologised when she realised the room lights were flashing so fast and changing colour so quickly it made us dizzy. We laughed and smiled.

We were definitely starting to get comfortable, but we weren't quite there. There was something in the air that I doubt either of us could put our fingers on, which made every action and sentence seem delicate. Second to the iPad, my favourite feature of the room was the floor-to-ceiling window framing the darkening cityscape.

On the other side, the city was still lighting up, coming alive for the evening. I always found London slow in this way. In Madrid and Paris, the transition from day to night seems to be completed over a matter of minutes.

Blinds open, I leaned on the largest pane in the centre to figure out where in the city we were. I hadn't been paying attention on the walk, which wasn't like me at all.

Usually my sense of direction is near-enough spot on. Talking to Megan had spun my inner compass. I'd lost myself to her. The view wasn't as impressive as the foyer may have led travellers to believe. It was mainly made up of the backs of office and tower blocks and the small concrete rooftop gardens of the houses on the opposite side of the street. Some were dotted with flowerpots. Others with chimneys. One was home to a man finishing a cigarette.

I watched as he flicked the butt onto the slated rooftop of the house below, the glowing ember rolling onto the level below.

"Damn," I said, "No sights here. You can't even see The Shard, which I think should be in that direction?" I squished my cheek against the window to look across the side of the hotel to see if I could glimpse it on the skyline. I've never loved architecture nor knew anything about it, but I've always had a fancy for old buildings. Especially French buildings.

There's something magical about walking through the streets of Paris, for example. It's a type of beauty I'm unable to put into words. Yet, while most modern buildings are fairly disgusting, a heavy mix of glass and metal, there's always something I can't quite put my finger on when I see The Shard. It's the exception to my rule.

Maybe because you can see it from so much of London, like a great big flagpole letting you know exactly where you are. I spoke about this once with Megan, trying to share the interest with her, but she said she was indifferent. They were just buildings, devoid of meaning. Built for function.

Here in the hotel, she still said nothing. I gave up on hunting for The Shard and glanced over at her. She had replaced the iPad with her phone, and it took a while for her to notice my gaze.

"Sorry, my friend is checking up on me. Making sure I'm okay."

"No problem." I smiled, heading towards and perching myself on the edge of the bed by her feet. She had fluffy polar bear socks on. "What did you say? 'Oh no, the guy's a creep. Can you get me out of here?'"

"I said he's way younger than me, and I don't know how to get out of it."

"Do you have an exit plan? You know, oh no, my friend was in an accident or her kitchen is on fire and I need to go. That kind of thing?"

"No. I'll just say I'm going to the bathroom and leave."

"Jesus. That's brutal. Although, I'd probably guess what's going on. You know the bathroom is literally just there, and I'm guessing you'd take your bag with you?"

"Hmm, okay, I'll leave my bag by the door just in case."

She faked getting up, and we laughed. Her smile

was so infectious. I could feel it warming my heart.

"What about you? What's your plan if things go south?" She asked.

"My exit plan? I've got a few, but it depends where we are and what we're doing. I've got my phone locked on the change ringtone screen for a quick exit, so I can just press play and say, " Oh, I have a phone call. Gotta go."

"That's much easier than texting a friend. What happens if they don't text back, right?" I got onto the bed next to her, leaving a little person-sized gap between us.

"So, which side are you on?" I asked, checking the pillow height and trying out how many stacked up pillows felt best. The hotel left five in total, all of which were massive. Even one put my head far higher up than I would normally sleep.

"Whichever. It's up to you. Which side do you want?" I turned towards the headboard and acted as though I was trying to work out some complex maths puzzle with exaggerated hand movements. Da-Vinci Code-styled.

"At home, I'm normally on this side, but near to the window, so that would make it this side, but you're already on this side, but the bathroom is there, so... Wait, how likely is it you're going to climb over me and go to the bathroom while we're asleep?"

"Extremely."

"Let's switch sides, then you don't have to climb

over me."

"Nah, I like that idea. I'll become a scuttling spider."

"The stuff of nightmares. Okay, well, I'm just going to have to take it from you."

I grasped Megan by the waist quite suddenly with both hands and tried to roll her over my side while tickling her to make her let go of whatever grasp she instinctively had on the bed or me. Her laughter filled my ears. I stopped quickly, not wanting to be too rough and found my face only a few inches from hers. Megan's expression remained neutral while catching her breath, but I could feel her heart beating through my chest. My ribs were vibrating with her life, her excitement. I could have moved my face forward no more than ten centimetres to kiss her, but I still couldn't do it. Fuck, I wanted to so badly.

She looked away, and I rolled off. A thought arose about how much disbelief I held at that moment. This girl I knew so intimately, this girl I had been talking to every day for the last month but hadn't actually met until this moment, was now lying in bed next to me, already fitting so comfortably. Kind of comfortably. Slowly, increasingly comfortably. I looked at her again. The silence hung. We didn't kiss. I wasn't confident enough.

Instead, I shifted positions back onto my side. No one said a word for several minutes. Still not right. My arm slid under the pillow and behind her head as I tried to gently usher her to roll over, seeing if she wanted to get close. Again, it was awkward. We both seemed a little spiky. We tried different positions, shifting around in silence. It just didn't want to work.

Forgiving the cliche, it was like trying to force together two jigsaw pieces that came from different sets. She shuffled and moved around. I twisted and turned in place.

One minute we would be close, half cuddling, my arms around her while she was tensed up into a little ball with her hands clasped together at her chest. Next, we were lying on our backs, staring at the ceiling or looking out the massive windows, commenting on how strange it was that you couldn't hear the traffic from the road below.

"I like the green light on that building." she pointed out to the horizon where a tower of some kind stood.

I could just make out the silhouette against the now night sky, the green light blinking at the top. Perhaps a warning light for planes, although they were usually red.

The city was now glowing with the artificial neon haze that London has. The transformation was complete. That glow beat across the ceiling, a sort of alien heartbeat. Eventually, I closed the curtains and turned the TV on at the wall.

"Fancy watching something? Maybe a film or an easy series?" I asked, picking up the iPad to flick through the apps. The charging stand beeped surprisingly, filling the air with a sudden, starling electricity when it was lifted from the stand. Had the room been that quiet? It felt as though this could have been the first sound we'd heard since closing the door.

"A series? Do we really have time?"

"I mean, if you have a favourite episode of something you want to watch or something like that? Silly. Or we can go and get food?"

"I'm not really hungry, I don't think." "How about we just watch something random and chill out?"

"Sure." She laid back a little more, dug her phone from underneath her and placed it on the bedside table. I sat back in bed and swiped across the screen of the iPad, dimming the lights slightly. While trying to find the perfect setting, I hit the romantic atmosphere setting, or 'mood', as it was listed.

No overhead lights, just a slight warmth as though a few candles had been placed around the outside of the room. The scene was complete and looked terrific with Megan lying on the bed. My imagination started to run of its own accord somewhere in the corner of my mind, and I panicked, turning the dial up to a brighter setting. I resisted the urge to look and see if Megan had felt the romantic setting too, but something told me she had.

Fuck, I can never recall overthinking so much in my life. Why do I do it so much now?

I swiped onto Netflix, and we decided to watch whatever came up on the front page. When it seemed like everything was working correctly and the sound wasn't too loud or too quiet, I threw the iPad to the side, jumping again at the alarming beep of the charging stand, and gracelessly made my way under the duvet.

Unconsciously, I made sure we remained a foot or so apart. The intro credits and logo rolled, and as soon as the first scene started talking about a bombing about to take place in Venice, my mind switched to zone-out mode. Did me and Megan work? Were we something that could happen? I couldn't remember a date with someone being this awkward ever before.

Then again, I'd never had a first date where we practically started it in bed together. And I never knew any other woman as well as I did Megan by the first date. It wasn't even awkward - that's the wrong word. It just felt... rigid.

We had both been stiff with nerves when we met. That was understandable. But still having them now? Should we be calmer? Are we calmer? Is that maybe because this meeting was so important? Had we made it this important? Why? Why did everything feel so fragile and delicate? So big. Where was the teenage innocence young lovers used to feel?

My nerves had basically dried up at this point, and I felt fine. A little overthinking, but okay. Yet Megan was still so reserved. So physically closed off. It made me nervous. Every part of her invited me to come closer, but when I got there, I met walls. We didn't fit together naturally.

Does that happen usually?

I couldn't remember it not happening with anyone else. Surely being close, cuddling or whatever, isn't this complicated. Maybe it was me, and she just wasn't noticing it? Was something wrong? Maybe we just weren't meant to be together?

Something in the movie exploded and caught my attention before I was dragged back into my thoughts several seconds later. I moved closer to Megan, more of an instinctual movement than a mindful attempt, and tried to find that perfect position without words, failed miserably, and went back to half-watching the movie a foot apart.

This repeating pattern continued for twenty or so painful minutes when we again shuffled around and forced ourselves to endure another unfortunate attempt at getting comfortably close. We shifted under the weight of each other, and without thinking, her lips found mine. In a heartbeat, everything fell into place.

Whatever fragments of nervousness we had between us, clinging to us, seemed to wash away like shore-crashed waves returning to the ocean.

8

The atmosphere in the room transitioned from tense to wholly comfortable, and, best of all, I could sense that Megan felt it too.

I could feel it on her lips.

Electricity coursed through her fingertips that ran over me. A surreal feeling of being inside a bubble swelled up around us. The rest of the world faded into the back of my consciousness and disappeared completely. With the sheets pulled up over our heads, we slowly took off our clothes down to our underwear and turned the lights down all the way. Kudos to the hotel; the romantic setting really was perfect.

Our hands and eyes explored each other's bodies in the gloom between kisses. Her touch was intense, her fingertips on my skin like tiny static shocks coursing through my nerves and into my very centre. With the hairs on my arms on end and my fingertips hypersensitive, I could feel her back glistening with goosebumps. I was content but at the same time wondering how far this was going to go.

Every second passed intensely. Every thought fleeting. Every feeling echoed like it had an infinite depth to it. I wanted to dive in. My mind kicked in. I knew from our recent conversations that Megan had been in some rough relationships in the past with exes who didn't understand 'no' or didn't care to understand it, so I knew that being intimate was something I had to be careful with.

"Hey, if you want to stop at any time, just tell me, okay?"

Megan nodded through the dark. Thoughts of sex itself had vanished completely. I didn't even want it. What I wanted was a way to express how intense a connection I felt at that moment. I don't think I'd kissed anyone the way I kissed Megan. She moaned and sighed between our lips touching, and we gasped while coming up from beneath the sheets for air.

Somehow I had found my way half on top of Megan. I started to kiss down her neck, pausing every couple of centimetres to gauge her reaction. I was careful. Slow. I couldn't bear the idea of crossing a line and ruining things forever.

With each kiss, she looked up towards the headboard, moaned softly, and made herself easier for me to kiss than before. We were synchronised. My lips continued to dance down her skin, across her chest, and over her stomach.

My hands ran gently down her shoulders and sides, over her hips and down her legs. I ran a single finger up the inside of her thigh, watching her face with complete presence. Yet as soon as my finger reached the top of her thigh, Megan's legs seized up, and her legs slammed shut, her hands covering her face.

"I'm sorry," she laughed, retreating into herself.

"I'm just nervous." I kissed her stomach once and sat up on my knees. The duvet fell. She took a deep breath and rubbed her eyes. Something exploded on the television behind me.

"It's okay. We don't have to do anything. Whatever you want."

I moved back up the bed and smiled. We kissed once and took a moment to close our eyes and reset. I took that moment to be with her, listening to her breathing.

"No pressure. Okay?" She nodded. I smiled to myself, feeling the sensations of warmth for a moment. Savouring what was happening. Bliss. When I opened my eyes again, Megan's face was in front of mine. I hadn't even felt her move. She moved in and kissed me, a kiss that was somehow ten times more intimate than before. I will never be able to explain how. How I had felt before paled in comparison.

The forcefulness of her lips confessed her comfort with me. With me and me alone. As did her hand sliding down my chest into my boxers.

Almost immediately, my hand followed suit, my fingertips moving carefully between her legs, our breathing heavier with every second that passed. We took our time, using our hands delicately while checking if everything was okay, yet we pushed further through the boundaries.

We both knew we could take our time. The urge to have my lips between her legs grew more intense, followed by a list of other wants and cravings, all of which stemmed from the desire to express how I was feeling inside. I didn't just want her physically. I wanted all of her. Everything she was.

At that moment, if I could have cut out both our souls and to let them dance freely for eternity, I'd have welcomed it. Perhaps that would be enough. It would indeed be a start.

I kissed down her body again, slid her underwear off gently with my teeth while smiling and kissing the inside of her thigh and put my lips between her legs. I paused, gently kissing her a little and looked up her body.

She was staring back down at me. A look flickered across her eyes before she smiled and nodded a little, her breathing still laboured, her hands pulling her hair up towards the headboard. Her head dropped back into the pillow as her eyes fell closed.

I slowly filtered down slight movements with my mouth and hands to see what she liked. Her attempts to stifle her moans failed. I loved that she couldn't contain herself and a huge sigh suggested she climaxed minutes later. I felt the urge to go again, silently asking through kisses. She curled up her legs and closed them around my head. Still, that felt hot, and I couldn't help but replay the memory of her coming repeatedly as though etching it into my brain. I wiped my mouth on the sheets and pulled myself up the bed next to her as she started to laugh.

"What?" I laughed back nervously, curious about what she found so funny. My ego verged slightly towards panic mode.

"I just, I don't even know," she said, her hands covering her face as she laughed harder and curled up into a ball surrounded by the scattered pillows and creased sheets.

"What?"

"That's probably the first time anyone has made me come without me, you know, having to help them. I can't believe you did that." I couldn't hide my smile.

"You're probably going to want to stop, or my ego's gonna get way too big." "No, but like wow. I was so nervous and when I'm nervous I can't, you know, finish. It's like it's too much pressure. That was good." She shook her hands as she spoke, as though drying them off after washing them.

"Shit. Well, I've set the bar now." I laughed and hated myself that nothing smoother was coming to mind. My wrists ached a ton though, and I may have strained my tongue if it's possible to do such a thing. I kissed her on the cheek. We lay in each other's arms for a few minutes before Megan moved her hand back into my boxers.

In unison, I slowly moved my hand back between her legs. We started gently, kissing each other a little. I bit her bottom lip, and we lost ourselves once again to heat, sweat, and short breaths. Megan's hand rubbed me hard, so hard I thought she would rip the skin off, but I was lost to it all.

We came within seconds of each other and fell back onto the bed, beads of sweat glistening in the city haze deeply cast across the room while listening to the sounds of our heaved breathing, the traffic outside, and a suitcase passing by the door in the hallway. The edges of the bubble faded, and we drifted back to reality. How I felt at that moment, I thought it was true love.

Whether it was or wasn't, I can't be sure, even now, but I know I had never felt anything like that before. I felt as though my life had direction, which was the start of something new. Life was beginning again. I was on my way out from wherever I was before that night.

The jury's still out on whether that's a good thing.

9

That night was the first time it happened.

I felt us succumb to the bubble that was us.

I later bought these feelings up months later, and she agreed she felt it too. A surreal feeling that the rest of the world had just slipped away, and we were the only ones alive. Spirits dancing in the void. We were there in our space. It's all we ever needed to be happy.

That delicate skin that surrounded us on our first night came to us repeatedly throughout the year. We lost ourselves to each other in this same way. It came out of nowhere, regardless of what we did. Any of the thousands of things couples do. Nothing beyond the limit mattered. Nothing else was real. There was nothing and nobody. Just me. Just Megan. Together.

Nothing could hurt us in those moments, and nothing could come between us. We were safe. We were calm. We could be ourselves without inhibitions.

We awoke in the hotel room to Megan's alarm the following morning and finished checking out within the hour. Megan took an early train to the conference in the south of the city. We parted ways just outside the hotel entrance, but there were no hugs or kisses. Just a nod and a smile. Still, I was elated from the night before.

On the train crossing the city to return home, I first took a step too far.

I had just felt so content. So in love or at least some version of it. Sunbeams shone through the train window. Its light warmed my face for what felt like the first time in years. I emerged out of the Underground, and feelings tugging my heart pulled stronger than I'd ever felt before. My world had changed. It was beautiful.

The ecstatic ripples of last night still flowed through every cell in my body. I was smitten. How amazing our time together in the hotel had been. It seems only logical that something terrible could have come from it. Yin and Yang. I text Megan trying to share at least a fraction of how I thought I felt.

I wasn't going to send it but wrote it in the Notes app of my smartphone. It read;

Hey.

Sorry if this is deep or whatever, but it's just what's on my mind. You don't need to reply if you don't want to. It's just a little something I thought I might share

This feeling of love I have for you is inescapable. It's consuming. This love bleeds through the barriers of consciousness and mindlessness. I feel like I've been loving you since we first started speaking, confirmed when we first met, and these feelings have made even the most mundane moments of my life seem bright and easy. I'm sitting on the train right now as I write this and feel like I must write this as I have no other outlet or way of expressing myself. I can't describe it.

I feel like I'm starting to understand the emotions of the millions before me who have declared love hurts just because I'm not with you. I'm listening to acoustic music for the first time in years, and the lyrics actually make sense. I feel sick, but I'm smiling.

You just sent me a single love heart in a message as I'm writing this, and it leaves me looking out the window, wondering if the sun has ever shone so bright. Has it always been this way? I'm falling.

I'm falling hard and fast, and I never want it to end.

The message felt stupid, but it came from the heart. I cringe now whenever I think about it. I thought the same when I read it back a few minutes later. That's why I locked the phone and decided to never think of it again. Until I did. I mean, why not send it? How could Megan not feel the same as me? What we had shared last night, what we had shared over the last month, it wasn't just lust. It couldn't be.

Off the text went. There was no response. Not that I blame her. The ice-cold blue ticks came up seconds after sending, and then she disappeared again. In the court of my mind, every possibility was bagged and presented as evidence. I was ghosted.

She'd met someone else at the conference. A cute guy, the rugby player type, said 'hey' on the train back up north, and that was it. She didn't like me. I'd done something wrong. We'd gone too far. The awkwardness at the beginning was too much. Maybe I should have sucked it up and kissed her goodbye. In some way, I'd ruined it all.

What did my future hold now? Several more years of waiting tables in a shitty restaurant surrounded by people who never look twice in my direction? My certain future time lapsed in front of me. Aaron moved out with Amy. I was left alone in a miserable flat with nothing but peeling walls and an inability to pay rent. I'd die in the winter with when the heating was shut off. No one would come to check to see if I was doing okay.

Or I'd grow old. The only people to reach out will be the phone lines set up to save older people from loneliness. I watched a few people get up and stand by the doors waiting to leave. I reminded myself not to be a victim. It's one message. She's at the conference. She's busy.

Yet still, even with internal reminders, every moment was spent combing over our conversations, word-by-word, from the moment we met to the moment I watched her walk down the road. Had she even turned back to see if I watched her walk away?

Hours turned to days. It felt like I was checking my phone every minute for a reply, every time surprised by how slowly the clock was creeping forward. Life was moving on. It took everything to resist the nearly overwhelming urge to call her. A soft voice in my head appeared from time to time.

Give her space. Don't be overbearing. I can be chill. Perhaps. Yet still, I spent so many moments checking social media to see if she had posted or quickly glimpsed when she had last been online. I was addicted -- telling myself I would wait, even putting my phone in my bag in the office, but always returning mid-shift after taking an order, the flipped, wire-coiled notebook still in my hand, to Megan.

From her Instagram page to the last place I had seen her - our text thread. The graveyard of our conversations.

On every visit, those blue ticks still glared at me. Piercing me. Like seeing the eyes of a gargoyle eternally perched on a podium. The eyes always fixed on the strangers, no matter where they stood.

The small grey text below her profile picture that would typically read online wasn't to be seen. It's so hard not to feel attached.

The cravings are so very real and so unavoidable. Willpower accounts for nothing when the cravings are for love.

10

I caved after a few days.

It was my first cigarette in months. While I had tried to talk myself out of it for my entire shift, the moment I passed the newsagents on the corner, I was in and out within minutes.

Flooded with guilt the second I sparked up. Felt sick on the first pull. The smoke was thick and suffocating. The taste revolting. I forced myself to keep going. The back of my throat found comfort in the breathlessness. Enough to take the edge off reality. I knew how closely that train of Thought resembled the acknowledged ramblings of an addict. Yet even with the edge smoothed and half a cigarette still to go, I caved and texted Megan asking if everything was okay.

I panicked.

Followed up with a second text; she didn't need to

reply. I just wanted to hang out again. I just wanted what we had before. To spend the evening lost together in our virtual world and video calls. My escape had escaped me. It took me by surprise when she replied seconds later by calling me. I threw the end of the cigarette and the rest of the pack down a passing drain set into the road before answering.

"Is that how you feel?" she said without a hello. Her voice was shy and quiet, as though she had been crying. A lump in her throat kind-of sound.

"With the text, I mean", she filled the silence I had yet to fill.

"Hey. You mean… you mean the one from the other day?"

"Yeah."

"I mean, yeah. I wrote it when I was on the train back after seeing you. I felt it then." I said. I wanted to try and play down how intense the message had been. I'd read it back countless times over the last couple of days, wishing there was a way I could un-send it.

"Do you feel it now?"

"Do I love you?"

"Yeah"

I paused. Moment of truth.

"Yeah, I think I do."

Fuck. What was wrong with me? If there was ever a way to scare someone off, this was it. An awkward silence followed. My mind was in full freak out panic mode. I found myself looking around, hoping a script might appear on the walls of the passing buildings or was scrawled across the pavement. There was a travel agent and a butcher. Both closed. I failed to find meaning in either. Megan said nothing.

I broke the silence with laughter that stemmed from the feeling of sudden clarity.

I might as well just speak from the heart. What was there to lose? Was I afraid of being ignored again? I had nothing to hide, so why not just lean into the truth completely? How

I felt was nothing to be ashamed of.

"I mean, of course, I love you," I said. "You've become such a big part of my life so quickly. I don't believe that means nothing. I don't even want to think about another version of my life where we didn't meet. I love having you around, and I love spending time with you. I love the idea of spending more time with you, so yeah, I think I love you. Maybe not in, you know, a soul mate, we're going to be with each other until we die kind of way, but to a degree. I mean, we have only met once."

That didn't feel too bad. At least it didn't until Megan continued to say nothing.

"It's okay," I said quickly to fill in the silence. "You don't need to say anything back. That's just how I feel. You can do what you want and make your own choices. Don't feel pressured to say anything. I'm just sharing my truth."

Silence again. I played with my nails, picking at

them, and didn't realise I'd crossed a road without looking either way until I'd reached the other side and a car passed quickly behind me. A little burst of adrenaline rippled through my heart. The side of one nail started to bleed a little. I sucked the blood off and quickly stuffed my hand into my coat pocket. The next moment, I found myself gripping the inside of my pocket, squeezing it tightly.

"You're just not my type," she finally blurted out of the nothingness. My stream of consciousness abruptly halted. Her words were sudden, much louder than I had ever heard her speak, but perhaps that was just by comparison to how quiet she'd been a moment ago. My face numbed, and eyes glazed over. I could see what was in front of me but simultaneously couldn't. My peripherals blurred by that single statement. Tunnel vision.

Another part of me, distant, was surprised. This was the reason why she hadn't been in touch? Another, perhaps wiser, part of my consciousness tried to remind me that everything was okay. This happens from time to time. This is life. It will be fine. Another part wanted to break down and cry.

Everything stung. The world around me faded, and even the sound of the passing cars felt a world away. I shook the fleeting thought of stepping in front of the next one to come along. I scared myself. My heart pounded louder in my chest. I said nothing and waited for more.

"I mean, the guys I've dated in the past, they've been very different. This, what we are, is all very new to me, and I don't really know where I'm at."

That's fair enough. I took a deep breath. "It's okay, I understand." I paused. What did I want to say? All I could think about was the eternal urge to be alone.

"I think I'm going to go. Don't worry, I'm not upset or anything, I just want to process for a bit. Got a lot going on in my head, you know? I'll speak to you later."

"No, Lucas, I didn't mean it like..." I hung up before she finished. I felt tears but held them back. I was hurt. Crushed. The night in the hotel had been magical. It was as though I was reborn. Reborn a million times over. A wise part of me kicked in. Stay rational.

I wasn't Megan's type. Simple. Sure, we got on talking online. We had fun playing video games and hanging out. Maybe that's all we were destined to be.

Just an escape for each other from the intense yet mundane realities we reside in. Perhaps we could go back there one day once the feelings had faded. That could work. I guess. I tried to formulate that in my head. I'd only known her a month. There's time.

By the time I got home, I'd downloaded Tinder; the rest of the evening then spent melted into my bed, swiping right on every possible profile with The Neverending Story playing in the background blurred.

I fell asleep just as the Rockbiter stared at his hands.

11

Nine days of radio silence passed before we text again.

I got in from work just after midnight but had left my phone in the bottom drawer of my bedside table for the shift. Checking was bordering obsessive. At this point, the idea of Megan and me had started to feel almost like a distant dream. Like one that had been so vivid the first few minutes of waking up, but now the details were obscured and faded. It was hard to recall the initial feelings. Checking was less an addiction and more a ritual. A private seance. The last remnants.

But still, even with a head of consciousness, I checked my phone the first moment I could. My heart swelled to see a text notification from her.

Lucas.

* * *

I'm sorry I've been distant. I just needed some time. Thank you for giving me space and being understanding. I know you're probably feeling shitty, and I've fucked everything up. I'm just not in a good place in general.

I had a really lovely time in London with you, but things are crazy and messy, and I didn't want to drag you into that. Everything you said scared me a little and made me shut down. I've got a lot of barriers up. I agree with everything you said about love, I think. I don't know. I just don't know how I feel anymore. I don't know who I am.

I'm always so numb, and life gets too much for me. I think we obviously connect, but we've only met once, so how could we possibly know we love each other? I don't even know what that feels like. I guess I just want to take things back. I'm sorry I've ruined everything.

I freak out like this sometimes. I'm sorry if I've hurt you. I understand if you don't want to speak with me. I just haven't had love in the way you see it. It's so romanticised. I don't know.

I'm sorry for everything.

All I could think to say was 'fair enough'. I read the message through several times before calling her.

"Hey," I started.

"Hey."

"I would ask if you're okay, but things are still crazy?"

"Er, yeah. A bit."

"Can I know what that means?"

"I don't know how to put it into words."

"Can you try?" I tried not to sound desperate, but all I had wanted for the last week or so was this conversation, and the aching inside was pleading to find out the truth.

"I don't know Lucas."

"Well, what did you mean by you're not used to this type of love?"

"Erm. Well, when I've been in other relationships, the guys have always been like, guy guys?"

"What, like rugby players, builder types that ride motorbikes?"

"Yeah, actually. Pretty much. I don't know."

"No, it makes sense. I mean, if that's your type, then that's your type." I sighed and caught a glimpse of myself in the black reflection of my bedroom window. Reality felt thick. Scrawny and thin. Shorter than most guys. Longish hair. Not a chance.

"No, it's not like that. Other guys have not been very emotional with me, not like you are. They were like, walls?"

"What does that mean?" I think I could tell, but I wanted her to say it out loud. I didn't want to assume anything at this point.

"I've always thought of myself being the romantic one in relationships. I would get home and make dinner for when he got home, and then we would watch TV in the evenings and yeah, that was nice. It was like the couples you see on TV. We would have sex and go to sleep. He would go out on Fridays with his rugby friends, and I would be there when he got home."

I could see the generic couple image in my mind's eye and couldn't help but react to it.

"No offence, but that sounds utterly horrible."

"It wasn't great. I just thought that was what romance was. I would tidy up and do everything nice like cooking and cleaning so he would be happy."

"You keep saying 'he'. Is there someone you're talking about specifically?"

"Kind of. I mean, all my exes have been like that really, so I mean them all."

"Okay."

"I don't know. I used to cry myself to sleep every night. I would try bringing up that I was sad, and it would just get shut down. I remember I bought this really sexy underwear online and..."

"Do I want to hear this?"

"Erm, I'll cut it down. So I bought underwear and did a dance when this one ex got home one day, and I wanted to take it all slow and make it all nice and everything was over in a few minutes., if you know what I mean. He just stuck it in and went to sleep."

I couldn't help but vividly imagine this happening; a mixture of imagination and memory created a tortuous image, but I couldn't make it go away until I caught my windowed reflection again. Seeing myself bought me back.

"Yeah. That really sounds horrible."

"I know. I tried bringing up that he just rushed it and wasn't thinking of me or us or anything, but he wouldn't have it. He said that my ideal romantic idea of love was just a fairy tale and didn't exist in real life. I guess since then I've just pushed it all down and told myself that's just how life is. This was just how relationships were. I've not known it to be any different."

"I'm sorry, but why would you put up with that? You do know you deserve so much more than that?"

I felt angry that Megan would have allowed herself to be treated in such a horrible way. Like an object. Just some part of some guy's life, like a sofa or a microwave. There when needed. Not a human being.

I couldn't imagine putting up with a relationship like that for even a second. I suddenly realised this was probably the first time she was ever talking about this out loud with anyone, and my mind shifted on this realisation. Compassion was essential.

"I'm sorry," I said, "I can see why that would seem normal if it's all you know. But if you don't want that and you know you're not happy, and you can see it, then why not change it? Be with different guys? And

I'm not just saying that to say be with me. I'm saying in general."

She took a moment to think before replying.

"Because it's secure. With these guys, yeah, it sucks, but I know exactly where I'm at and what's happening. They're not going to leave me. Everything's stable. I know that sounds stupid, but all I've wanted in life is to be a mum. I have this idea of having a family and having kids, and it's not until recently that I've realised I've never really cared who the guy was in the picture. I only ever thought about it being me and some kids."

"And some animals. Probably horses." She had been crying a little while speaking, but with that one sentence, she laughed. I smiled at my reflection. I smiled back.

"Yes. And animals too."

"I mean, you don't need to think that's weird. It makes a lot of sense that you want that stability. I doubt a guy would leave you if you were basically looking after him, and he could give you the kids you've always imagined."

"Fuck Lucas. That sounds so fucked up. Not caring who the guy was. Imagine if I had married one of those guys."

"I'm not saying anything. But yeah, if you did, then I would feel very sorry for you if I ever met you." I tried to make that sound as light-hearted as possible, despite it being a hard truth.

"Yeah. Me too. I think it's just that there were no surprises with those guys. It sucked a lot, but it was all so straightforward and simple."

"Yeah, I can't say I'm a massive fan of simple relationships," I admitted.

"Yeah. You're complicated and emotional. I can't imagine having this conversation with any of them. They would just never open up about any of it. But at the same time, they would never even ask me how my day was. It's like opposite ends of the scale."

"I suppose I did just tell you I loved you after meeting you once."

"Yeah, exactly! What a bombshell! Can you see why it took me by surprise?"

"I can. I'm sorry I just unloaded it on you, but it's how I feel. And just as a side note, I love your romantic view of love. The house. The animals. The garden. Kids running around and making dinner for them and all that. I get it and I love it. I'm sure if you genuinely want that kind of life, then you'll get it one day. I will say that you should probably find a guy who you actually enjoy being with though, seeing as though you'll be starting a life with him." We both laughed.

"Yeah. I can't believe I've never thought of that before. I just desperately wanted this idea in my head and didn't really care how to get it. Although I obviously do because I was so sad being with them. Can I be honest though?"

"Of course."

"It was a little heartbreaking when you hung up on me the other day after we called. That's another reason why I feel like we're unstable. One second we're talking and then you're hanging up and I don't know where you are or if we're talking or whether I should text you or how long to wait. Situations like that make me go kind of crazy."

I thought for a moment.

"I get it. I did say I just wanted some time to process what you were saying. I was angry and upset and didn't know what to say, so I just wanted the space."

"You were angry? Why?"

"Do you want to tell someone you love them with all your heart only to be told you're not their time? What do you expect me to be? Excited?"

"Well no. I just didn't know you felt angry."

"Okay, maybe angry was a strong word. I was just upset and emotional. You're right. I just needed some time."

"Yeah. I'm sorry."

"Me too. One second, I'm just getting some water."

I put the phone down and took a moment to breathe.

For Megan, love was routine. Stability. For me, excitement. Uncertainty. One of us had to be wrong. It would take time to process. I paced around the room several times before picking the phone up.

"Hey. I'm back."

"Hey."

"Did you know it's like 2am?"

"Fuck. Where does the time go?"

"I know right?"

"I spent all evening on the phone with Daisy this evening trying to figure out what to say to you. I actually have a Post-It note here with some notes on it."

"Oh really? What bullet points do you have? God, you're such a paperwork freak. To-do lists even for conversations like this. Have you ticked everything off Miss?" I teased her and we both laughed.

"Har har. Very funny."

"Well, I think I'm going to go to bed cos this is all way too much for my head and I don't think I can go on anymore." "Yeah, me too. I can hardly keep my eyes open."

"Want to stay on the call?"

"For sure." My phone buzzed and Megan was turning the phone call into a video call. I accepted and propped the phone up on the stack of books next to my bed. The room was silent apart from the soft hum from the microphones but was broken one last time before drifting off to sleep.

"Lucas?"

"Yes, Megan?"

"I love you too."

I smiled in the darkness and made the sound of blowing her a kiss. The words meant so much and were exactly what I wanted to hear the entire time, but they still cut something inside.

Perhaps love's a word that means something different every time we let it out.

12

Three months passed.

Everything was great.

We spoke over the phone or by video nearly every day.

Most evenings were spent taking turns to read to each other until the other fell asleep. We lost ourselves to our video game or endless hours faded with chatting about everything and anything.

We shared hopes and dreams for the future and our perspectives on the world. I loved hers. She was just so passionate about so many things. She loved nature and being out in the wilderness.

She'd indulged in a love for landscape photography for a few years, only giving it up when work demanded too many hours.

She loved concepts like sustainable living, the idea of

being vegan, and recycling junk and up-cycling old furniture. She planned to volunteer her time helping the elderly or less fortunate people someday.

Yet it was all unmanifested. While she held all these passions and ideas, they were just that. Ideas. I asked several times why she didn't actually spend some of her time doing these things.

I'd suggest taking trips out with her camera to photograph some places in the city, or joining a volunteering scheme. I always tried to keep the conversations as inspirationally as possible, hoping that I myself would also heed this advice. No one wants to be stuck in a dead-end job with no aspirations and no hopes for the future.

Maybe I'd motivate myself to practice what I preached.

"I will," she would say. "I just want to get my head in the right place first."

As days turned to weeks turned to months, we grew closer. Megan's barriers continued to fall. I sensed it. I began to see more of her. The real her. Since the day we crossed paths, I'd always thought of Megan as a dreamer, gliding through life, moving with flow, but the actual reality was a little different. She was undoubtedly more human.

Most days, she struggled with the pressures of university. Her relationships with peers. Her slavedriver of a supervisor she didn't know how to deal with. I also found out that of the four boyfriends of her past, she was still in contact with all of them, in one way or another.

The classic sharing of romantic pasts, as people do. Curious as to who new loves have spent their time on. The joys they shared. What went wrong. There are always answers to our innermost questions in that part of our lives. How could there not be?

Megan would speak of them all from time to time, sometimes when a memory triggered or recounting a story about a time gone past. Maybe a mention of a vacation, a trip to the mountains for a weekend of photographing, or getting called into the office at university.

Perhaps the reason I felt so unsettled by this news was the fact she had recently broken up with her previous ex a week or so before we met online. She spoke of how he couldn't seem to leave her alone and messaged weekly.

She'd reply every now and then. She checked another ex's Instagram daily. I could never pinpoint why it made it feel so uncomfortable, having the past hang around with the present in such a way.

Perhaps a taboo feeling. Jealousy? Curiosity?

She said they were friends. Two of them were dating other people whom she caught up with every so often.

Another ex drifted in and out of her messages every now and then, usually no more than a few messages with months of time in-between. The most recent ex, Matthew, was plain annoying.

He was married. Wife. They had a son together. They were going through a divorce that had lasted over a year and was still ongoing. He and Megan had met during the start of divorce process, and, judging by the texts Megan sent me to read from him, he was simply using her to rant about the whole thing.

She said she hated it. Felt used but never told him to stop. I questioned it a few times, but the conversation led nowhere and the topic ended up drifting by the wayside. As I stood on the rooftop of my apartment, daybreak faded out the night as cigarette smoke curled in the morning breeze. Never a better time for thinking.

For me, relationships came and went. If they weren't meant to be, they weren't. Take the lessons learned and move on. It wasn't intentionally like that, but just the way my past relationships had panned out. They barely lasted longer than a few months.

That was just the way life naturally unfolded. She didn't seem to think it strange having fragments of past lives linger in the shadows.

"Don't you think it's a waste?" She explained. "You spend all this time getting to know someone and making all these memories and then it all just disappears and fades away. Just feels like a waste of time if it turns into nothingness."

Despite Megan's struggles, my life had developed a kind of meaning and purpose. In hindsight, I tell myself this and it sounds incredibly messed up. I see it now, but that's how I felt at the time. I'd been drafted by love and spent my days carrying out acts of service.

When Megan succumbed to a stressful day or felt overwhelmed for no notable reason, we'd call. I'd convince her to get into bed, watch her take her antidepressant, then read our book until she fell asleep. Sometimes I would order an UberEats care package.

I liked being supportive of the girl I loved. To support her when she needed someone there. When she needed me. It was hard.

With her living up in Edinburgh and I in London. Four hundred miles and eight hours of train tracks apart. It was difficult not being able to be there for her in the way I wanted to be. I craved being at her house when she finished at the office, fish and chips warming in the oven, a bubble bath with candles topped up ready.

I did the best I could with long sweet messages and positive affirmations that everything would be okay. We spent hours inside the League world, but admittedly, our fun chases around the map, not caring whether we win or lose, had turned into bitter losses and mindlessly clicking. We played without saying a word to each other for minutes at a time.

We held on for a chance to meet in person again. I was convinced everything would be okay.

We'd surely click back into place when we finally got to be physically together once more.

13

Life threw curveballs. Cracks appeared.

Due to reasons unknown, the restaurant made cutbacks, closing the quieter days of the week and I found myself without work multiple nights of the week. To afford rent, I'd stopped going out a month or so beforehand anyway but had to still take up a temporary second job.

Opportunities felt limited, and I quickly found myself on the night shift of a beer bottling factory. The role was simple. Stand in the same spot on a conveyor belt in a windowless factory, making sure none of the bottles passing by me hadn't fallen over. If, lo and behold, they had, I uprighted them. It wasn't the most engaging 12-hour shift, but needs must.

Most nights were the same. Hours spent surrounded by Polish agency workers who spoke little English, not that any conversation could make it above the raging of the machines. Instead, I would keep my phone in both hands just below the edge of the belt, texting Megan or scrolling mindlessly.

One unspecific night, the hours were spent trying to calm Megan down from a panic attack. She said she'd been made responsible for compiling a report for something. A report she couldn't figure out the context for and it sent her spiralling.

"I can't do it. Everyone's going to be so mad at me. What if I let everyone down? This is stuff I should know."

"Megan. Take a deep breath. You've got this. Where did you put the red folder they gave you?"

"I don't know! Fuck. I'm going for a walk."

"Megan, it's nearly midnight. Just go and stand outside? Get some air."

"I'll text you later."

Amongst the intensity, a couple of fallen bottles had slipped past my sentry and were now causing havoc at the filter a few metres down, a spot where the conveyor belt merged into a thinner, single-file line. Bottles were building up, endless glass pillars falling on collision.

Of course, I was obliterated by the floor manager. Not only for the pile-up that now needed sorting, but for a complete disregard for the factory's health and safety policy. In the true authoritative tone of a factory pit bull, I was deemed lucky not to be fired on the spot. Perhaps he was waiting for the problem to be sorted first.

I was forced to stop texting without warning.

I didn't hear from Megan. I text a few times explaining what happened. A few more times out of the anxiety of being abandoned. Then I left it. I was getting better at just leaving the situation alone to breathe.

At some point in the afternoon of the third day, I was standing in a bookshop, in the travel books section, staring mindlessly at the messiest rainbow of colourful spines before me. I had no intention of buying anything. Come to think of it, I don't even recall getting there in the first place or why I was out in the city to begin with.

My phone pinged as my eyes skimmed the tales of motorbike adventures along African highways and Lonely Planet guides on Japan. Megan. A message full of confusing non-sequiturs.

There was no sense of what she was trying to say. We went back and forth several times, generic eggshell messages saying I was okay and had been mostly busy with work and sleeping.

Yet every reply was a cocktail of asking how I was repeatedly and clearly having something she wanted to talk to me about, yet she never entirely made it to the point. Something felt off. I left the store, headed in a direction unknown, and called to find out the truth.

"Lucas. I'm really sorry."

"You're sorry? For what? Megan. Just tell me."

Silence.

"I can tell something's wrong. Just tell me what it is. Why won't you tell me where you've been the last few days? I've been so worried. Have I done something wrong?"

"No. It's not that."

"Megan. Enough with the cryptic messages."

"Okay. Okay. Just give me a second."

"Sure."

I held my breath and tried to remain patient. My mind raced.

"The other night. My head was going crazy and I couldn't sleep. I couldn't stop crying." She took a long deep breath, her exhale causing the microphone to static slightly before continuing.

"I was so scared I was going to cut myself. It's like I couldn't think about doing anything else. It was like I had tunnel vision. All these thoughts in my head just wouldn't stop."

"Oh, baby. I think I knew by your tone of voice. But you've been like it before. Are you okay? Did you, you know, do it?"

"No, I didn't."

"That's amazing, sweetheart! I know those urges can be so strong, so you should be really proud of yourself for getting through it. I'm proud of you. I'm also really sorry I couldn't be there. The boss was being such a dick..."

"Lucas." Megan cut me off. She started to cry. "I was so scared of being alone and doing it. I didn't want to be by myself."

"Okay?"

"Fuck. Okay, I'm just going to say it. I called Matthew. I asked him to come over that night. I'm so sorry. I didn't know who else to call. I felt so horrible. I just needed some company."

"Wait. Okay, I get that you didn't want to be alone, but you called him? Him of all people?"

"I was going crazy. I didn't know what else to do."

My mind was racing to the point I felt dizzy. If I had held my breath, I could probably have passed out. It took every ounce of energy to be as reasonable as I could be. My stream of thinking swayed from being compassionate and understanding to wanting to say some incredibly nasty things I found myself shocked at for even thinking.

"Okay. Fine. Doesn't matter; he was your ex. You just needed someone to be there for you to be grounded. That's all right?"

"I didn't mean for it to happen."

"So you slept with him?"

Megan said nothing. Her silence confessed it.

"What the fuck? How do you go from feeling like life isn't worth living and wanting to cut yourself to suddenly being in the mood? Please, enlighten me. Tell me how that works."

"He just came round. I said I was having a bad time

and wanted some company. We watched a movie and it just happened. I literally don't even know how it happened. It just did. I'm so sorry. I wish I could go back in time and undo it."

I couldn't even bring myself to say anything. I couldn't think. All I had when it came to what Matthew looked like was an old photo Megan had shown me on her phone of him helping her change a tyre on her car.

I pictured them watching a movie on opposite ends of the sofa. I watched them get closer. I watched her crying in his arms. She looks up, wipes the tears away and kisses his jawline just under his mouth. He looks down, curls a finger under her chin and pulls her closer for a kiss.

The next moment, they're standing in front of each other, clothes screwed up at the foot of the coffee table. They take a step closer to one another. Another. Another. They're in each other's arms. She's pushed up against the back of the sofa, her knees sinking into the cushions, his hands around holding her hips. She's moaning his name.

I choked a little. Livid at my own mind for betraying me. Why? Why are you showing me this?

One part of me understood. If I'd been in her position, I'd have wanted an escape too. Anything to stop the thoughts. Megan patched the silence.

"Lucas. I asked him to leave as soon as I could and he did. I felt so guilty. I've wanted to tell you for days. I just haven't been able to do it. There's just so much pressure to live and stick to these rules and be someone for everyone else and I can't take it."

"Sorry, but what the fuck are you talking about? Being someone for someone else? Just be you. Be yourself. That's all anyone can ever ask. Is that why you were feeling stressed in the first place? I don't get what you're saying."

"There's so much pressure. All the time. Everyone expects me to be this person who can do it all. Any time someone needs something done, they can rely on me. I'm that person. It just gets a little much."

"Yeah, no shit. No one can be there all the time for anyone. You've got to make sure you're taking breaks. Your health has to come first. If you're not looking after yourself properly, you can't show up in the world as the best version of yourself, hell, even a semi-decent version of yourself. You're allowed to take time away. Everyone understands that, even if they don't make it feel like that. You don't have to pretend to be anything."

"You don't understand. My parents think I'm this high-flying academic destined to do great things and change the world. I have to make them proud. My supervisor wants me to be top of the class. You want me to be a good girlfriend. I have to do these things, and I keep messing them up."

"What are you talking about? You're telling me you're pretending to be someone else to try and please everyone else in your life and getting so stressed about it that you end up wanting to cut yourself and sleep with your ex? What good do you think that's doing anyone, especially yourself? You know you have way more control over things than you think?"

"I told you. My head isn't in a good place. I don't know who I am. I don't know who I want to be. This time last year, I was happy being sad. I know that sounds stupid, but I knew where I was. I knew my role in life, and now that's gone. I'm lost. I've lost myself."

I took it all on board and listened. It hurt a lot. Obviously. As much as I resisted, I mentally tortured myself with details of her sleeping with Matthew. I envisioned what the room looked like. What positions they had twisted and turned in. I imagined her moans and what facial expressions she would have made. I couldn't help myself.

My mind added extra vivid details every time it looped back around to the start of the scene. Then, without warning, a drip of compassion splashed across my consciousness. I sighed and tried to reset.

"Everything's okay Megan. It's okay. I really appreciate you telling me what happened. I'm sorry I got angry. It can't have been easy. Obviously it hurts, but what's done is done. If I'm going to get over it, it's just something that will take time."

"Yeah."

"You were just struggling and in a bad place and you

had to use a coping mechanism to deal with it. That's understandable. Everyone has coping mechanisms."

"Yeah. I'm sorry. I don't know why mine have to be that. I just..."

"It's okay. You don't have to explain anything." We said a few short statements to each other and I told her I planned to sleep off everything that had happened. She agreed. I watched the tiny green dot of her online status turn red, then grey as she went offline. My phone screen turned black.

Stuffing it back into my pocket, I found my way to the nearest store.

Inside, I bought the same brand of B&H Golds cigarettes I always smoked and sat on the thin wooden ledge out the front of the store and smoked one after another until evening consumed the city in darkness.

14

Megan spontaneously booked a rather expensive cottage for a weekend away.

Although it was never directly stated, I always believed it was her way of saying sorry. The cottage was located in a remote yet naturally stunning part of northern Scotland, a few miles outside the town of Aviemore, right next to the famous Cairngorms National Park. It's a kind of beautiful I never expected to find in the UK.

I had no say in the matter. It was incredibly remote and romantic, and I'd been excited from the moment she told me it was booked. It started out as a surprise trip, but not as much as I'd been told minutes after booking that something was happening, but it involved a cottage. I just didn't know where it would be until the day we went. She told me all the details before the day was over.

I didn't care. I pushed the thoughts of what happened with her and Matthew and the stresses of the past few weeks to the back of my mind and focused on the positive future we were heading into. It's strange to think that this was the second time we'd see each other face-to-face after being together for months.

A chance for just us to hide away from the world for a few days.

I took the train up to Edinburgh on the Thursday and arrived at her house just before 10pm.

15

Megan had already taken a Quetiapine before I got off the train and was half asleep by the time I arrived, so her housemate, Abby, opened the door.

Megan had only spoken of Abby on a few occasions, and from what was spoken, they were friends, but they weren't close. Abby was studying marine biology. It had something to do with coral reefs, but it was incredibly scientific, and I didn't understand much. Abby was also very proactive when it came to attending clubs and being a part of the communities run at the university. This included her being a member of the canoeing club, golf club, running club, and debate club and organising many trips for elderly people to go all over the country, which she would help supervise on the weekends.

Stepping into the kitchen, Abby had sat at the table

with the dimmers turned low, a candle on the table, and soft Lofi jazz playing in the background. She stood aside to let me in, looked me up and down, and leaned against the kitchen worktop. It was lovely for a student house, so much so I was led to believe it wasn't student accommodation at all. I later found out it was a house Megan's family owned, and Abby paid rent.

The kitchen was incredibly well-organised and tidy. The fridge-freezer was full of magnets collected from holidays, timetables with chores divided up between Abby and Megan, and a photo of them in a European cafe. The style made me think it was Italy.

We made small talk about the train journey up and how Scotland was already cold despite being September before Abby excused herself to make a call in the front room. Megan had already explained the layout of the house. Abby had the rooms downstairs, and Megan was upstairs. I crept up, quickly found her bedroom, placed my bags in the corner of the room, being very careful not to wake Megan, and edged myself into bed.

She stirred a little and we kissed sleepily, cuddled for a bit, but Megan was soon back out for the count entirely. I quietly watched The Office US on my phone until I fell asleep.

Hours later, the alarm went rang. I leaned in for a kiss and shuffled closer for a morning cuddle. It blew my mind that I was here, in her space, together. We had been waiting for the right time to meet up and spend some quality time together for months, and now here we were.

The early morning sunlight beamed through the blinds, and the scene with her was once again like being a part of a movie. Life felt cinematic. I looked at her and just felt so full.

There's no other way to describe it. There was so much love inside me at that moment I felt like I could explode. I looked at her. It felt as though I was looking at her properly for the first time. I could see all the nuances of her face crystal clearly in a way I had never done before. The waves of her hair. The way the light bounced off and warmed her skin. The colours. The spread of goosebumps on her arm as I lifted the sheet. Her smell. My senses were alive.

I found it hard to believe she actually existed. This moment surely couldn't be real. Having her in front of me was like being presented with a treat I didn't deserve.

Megan woke in a shitty mood.

Her back was to me as I leaned over to kiss her cheek, and she didn't move a muscle. I was a little stunned that she blankly ignored the gesture, choosing instead to continue scrolling on her phone.

"Morning," I said, "how long have you been awake?"

"A while." I stole a glance at her phone.

She seemed to have received an email from her course supervisor, Lisa, saying she had a ton of edits on her latest paper. In that moment, even just through a quick scan of the words, something clicked. I could feel the stress and tension oozing from her pores. A thick and unwanted substance slowly filled the room, forcing out all the oxygen. Filled the air between us so we couldn't possibly be close. It was as though a dark tar had been silently dripping through the ceiling all night.

"Are you okay?" I asked.

"Yeah, just tired." She noticed me looking over her shoulder. "And just got an email from Lisa."

I nodded and lay back down. Megan rolled onto her back to stare at the ceiling, cracking an obviously fake half-smile. I attempted to kiss her on the cheek again, but that was apparently too far.

She made that clear by sitting on the floor on the other side of the room next to her chest of drawers. She then started to pull clothes out of them without saying a word.

"What's up?" I asked as she pulled out socks and underwear before leaning across the floor to grab an empty rucksack propped up against the wall next to the door.

"Nothing."

"That's entirely convincing. You can tell me you know."

"No. Nothing. Everything's fine."

"Is it about your paper? You know Lisa won't be in the office until Tuesday morning, so you don't have to worry about it until then?"

"I know."

"But?"

"But nothing."

"If you want to leave a little later today and work on your paper, we can. Or we could even go tomorrow to give yourself some time, I don't mind you know. I can find something to do online on my phone. It could be like our own little study group."

"Everything's fine. I'll deal with it on Monday."

"Okay. If you're sure."

I wasn't convinced. Her blank expression told me she wasn't either. I took her clearly unaffectionate manner personally for about a second, but a voice in the back of my mind nagged, reminding me Megan wasn't a morning person.

She'd be stressed about packing for the weekend and the work she had just been set. I knew Megan well enough at this point to know she would instead love to get everything done and her to-do list items ticked off and out of the way before any of the expected niceties could commence.

A bitter voice behind my voice of reason called her a bitch and couldn't believe we wouldn't start our romantic weekend without romantic morning cuddles.

The voice was silenced just as quickly as it had appeared by Cinnamon, her cat, jumping up onto the bed and falling over on her side, eagerly awaiting a tummy rub. A gorgeous cat, Cinnamon was clearly a

Maine Coon although cross-bred with something else. I asked, but Megan flat-out ignored the question.

I cuddled and pet Cinnamon while taking in the bedroom properly for the first time as Megan went downstairs to make breakfast and pack the rest of her things. The room was fairly minimal. The walls were bare, with a few photos hanging up in fancy wooden frames that created a linked pattern. Nothing with any real personality.

Her bed was double my size and gave way to a surprisingly stunning panoramic view of the city since it backed onto the window. It felt abnormally quiet compared with the bustle of London, but then we were quite a way from the city centre. I shooed the cat away and got up upon hearing the toaster pop downstairs.

I half-smiled as Megan drank tea at the table, ate toast, and scrolled on her phone. She didn't look up as I helped myself to bread and orange juice from the fridge. Thanks for offering, Megan.

We ate quietly at the kitchen table, made small talk with Abby as she left for a bike ride with her boyfriend, checked our bags over one last time - mine was still packed from the night before - and set off, cottage-bound.

The first stop, however, was a supply run to the supermarket. The bitterness that had built up over the morning seemed to fade quickly as we rode in the car, which was another surprisingly nice and expensive addition to her life. A BMW off-road thing. Not a massive truck, but still clearly a 4x4, in an infinitely deep black. I wasn't a car person, but I could tell this was relatively new. I played with the touchscreen media centre in the dashboard, copying the cottage's postcode from a booking reference she'd printed off.

"It was a gift," Megan said, as though reading my mind. "My ex upgraded and gave me this instead of swapping it. His parents are rich."

Perhaps the morning had simply been a glitch. A minor hiccup that could and should be forgotten about just as quickly as it arose, like a worrying pang of the heart that creates fear of a heart attack but is gone and forgotten about within minutes of its arrival. Solemn moods turned into bouncy steps through the car park and along the supermarket aisles with this frame of mind.

Steps accompanied by the random throwing of unessential items into the basket and being overly flirty once Megan had let slip that she knew people who worked in the store and didn't want to be seen in that way so publicly.

Naturally, a mention of this fear only provoked me to exaggerate it, in a fun way of course. I skipped before her, nudged her with the trolley, tried to hold her hand and sang along to the music played out of the speakers overhead. Megan simply wasn't in the mood.

I was messing around and I didn't do anything I would personally deem as 'crossing the line' of PDA.

Yet, with every ignored action, whether it be a joke, a peck on the cheek, or an opportunity to dance in front of the tea bags, I began to sting once again.

It was as though thousands of tiny little paper cuts uncomfortably yet fleetingly sliced me up on the inside.

16

The ride to the cottage changed little.

Megan drove silently, supposedly lost in thought while I danced in the passenger seat to club music and attempted to catch M&Ms in my mouth. Megan slowly began to subtly nod her head to the repetitive bass lines after an hour on the road.

"Sorry," I said, reaching out for the radio's dials. "I can turn it off if it's distracting."

The car started to rumble as we drifted into the hard shoulder. Megan jerked the car back into the middle of the lane abruptly, but her look remained unchanged.

"No, it's fine. Sorry. I'm just tired."

"Are you sure? I mean, we did nearly skip a red light earlier."

"Yeah. No. It's fine. The music is keeping me

awake."

"If you're sure."

Whether a distraction for Megan or not, I knew that's what the music was for me. The peaking drops of each track took me back to music festivals with friends where I danced all day in the baking summer sun, took pills with strangers in front of the fantastic bands and DJs on the main stages, and got high in the campground and forests of whatever park we were in with new and old friends alike.

I smiled to myself on that Scottish road as I watched families sitting quietly in the cars we overtook, trying to ignore the unrealistic amount of affection Megan wasn't giving me.

We reached the cottage mid-afternoon. It was beautiful.

Sat at the end of a mile-long dirt track bordered by a line of trees, then foggy fields of sheep, which were bordered themselves by snow-capped mountains and chilling grey skies. It was exciting, especially since we'd both crossed our fingers for snow. It felt as though I hadn't seen snow in years, what with climate change and London's hot concrete streets.

The gravel track crunched under the car as it opened up at the end to reveal a quaint white bungalow with plants in red, shiny ceramic pots posted next to the door and besides the windows, as well as in the bright overhanging timber porch.

The owner, Robert, an elderly man in his 60s who

lived in the cottage next door, welcomed us and took us on the tour.

He handed us a posh-looking wooden folder containing laminated information sheets printed with instructions and tips for where everything was and how the house amenities worked, all typed in a handwritten font.

We followed him into the kitchen where he shared excessive detail on where everything was kept. He showed us how to use the sauna in the bathroom, the hot tub outside on the decking, and where the wood for the wood burner could be found just outside the back door.

As we walked from room to room, I tried to think of a realistic number representing how human beings were conceived within these walls. I reckoned forty.

The hour or so it took to settle in after Robert left wishing us a happy stay was mostly spent sorting out our bags and unpacking our clothes onto the chairs next to each side of the bed.

Megan was practically silent, occupying herself with an expedition to the cupboards in the bathroom and kitchen. After giving myself another quick tour, taking a few photos for Instagram in the process, I offered to cook dinner and suggested that maybe Megan could take a shower to wake herself up.

Still looking completely dazed, she agreed and plodded back into the bedroom while I dived into our supplies. Lots of vegetables, noodles, and sauce. A stir-fry as planned. It was always my go-to meal since it never took long and always tasted amazing. One could never go wrong with a stir-fry.

As soon as I heard the sounds of the water cascade into the shower tray, I made my way around the main living space to try and make everything look as inviting as possible, which wasn't hard since Robert had clearly taken the time to make the rooms as romantic-looking as possible.

Everything was mostly cream-coloured, thrown with colourful blankets and cushions. Abstract, erotic artwork hung on every wall. Every ledge and smaller window sill was covered with an array of scented candles.

There were extra-soft blankets for hanging out in front of the fire under, various board games stacked under the TV, and even pairs of fluffy slippers. I quietly lined the hallway from the bathroom door to the wood burner with tea lights from a bag stored under the kitchen sink. I then attempted to light the wood burner but realised I'd never really used one before.

It took two attempts to successfully nurture the small flame of a match to turn into a roaring inferno, leaving me feeling much more manly than usual. I smiled to myself in the quiet room, enjoying the crackling of the fire.

For a moment, I felt content. The shitty morning and the tense car ride seemed almost distant.

With snow starting to fall outside and the warmth of the fire slowly warming the room, it felt nice. I noticed the soft classical music coming from a radio somewhere behind the television unit through the peace. This radio or CD must have been playing since we arrived, but had no idea where the sound was coming from or how to turn it off. Still, it was an excellent addition I wouldn't have thought of.

The finishing touch was throwing one of the biggest, fluffiest, most premium-feeling white blankets I had ever had the pleasure of touching out in front of the fire, stripping off my clothes, and then lying on it naked, a corner of the blanket folded over to hide my waist.

I know it sounds a bit like a movie cliche, but that's the cheesy look I was going for.

I think both me and Megan needed a bit of fun. The bathroom door opened, my signal to position myself in the best, hopefully most attractive, way possible.

I found a lovely position on my side with my leg cocked up, knee pointing towards the ceiling, but quickly realised I was too close to the wood burner as my skin started to warm up and burn rapidly.

I shuffled myself and the blanket in the opposite direction at the last minute, desperate not to seem suspicious by making too much noise. Was I going to come off as an awkward mess or a romantic hero?

Either way, it was too late to back out. My mind left my worries to the side as Megan came into the room, floating down the candle-lit hallway with a hand on her heart, smiling. She sighed. As she came closer, I felt our bubble enveloping us and awareness of the rest of the world fading away like the smoke being sucked gently up the chimney.

Everything, from the foreplay to the climax, was intense. We didn't have sex. I went down with my mouth between her legs. Her skin was warm from the fire and shower, and she smelled of fruity shower gel.

Her orgasm rippled through her whole body, causing her to spasm in my arms, her hands pulling hard on my hair, my hands on her hips, trying to keep her in place.

Afterwards, she lay down next to me, still catching her breath, and held my penis in her hands, caressing the tip softly with her fingers. We kissed a little and listened to the fire crack beside us, the heat embracing our bodies and tickling our skin. I kissed her forehead, and we lay for a few minutes longer in still silence.

No thoughts. No worries. I was relaxed. So relaxed, I started to go soft in her hands, but that didn't matter. At least it didn't matter to me.

In a quick movement, Megan noticeably panicked and started to move her hands to make me hard again. Her hand movements made her panic so clear that it didn't have the desired effect.

"It's okay. You don't have to. I'm okay." I said. It was too late. Megan darted.

"I'm going to go and get dressed," she said abruptly,

standing up, the white fluffy blanket dropping. I silently watched as she quickly wrapped herself back up in her original towel that had been cast away by our feet.

Before I even had a chance to reply, she disappeared off into the hallway, the walls still flickering with the soft glow of the tea lights. Overwhelming feelings kept me quiet and reserved.

They lasted longer than Megan spent dressing, and we barely spoke to each other for the rest of the evening.

I tidied all the romantic props away and was nearly done cooking before Megan returned. I finished up and served while Megan played on her phone across the room on the sofa in front of the TV and said the bare minimum while choosing something to watch on Netflix while we ate.

To my surprise, Megan actually hinted at playing one of the board games in the cabinet underneath the television after I had washed up, but I shrugged the idea off without saying much. I was torn.

One half of me would have loved to play a board game, hopefully indulging ourselves in an opportunity to connect.

That's where my heart wanted to be. Another part of me felt as though this would only open the gateway to experiencing further disappointment the moment I let my guard down. Megan was the one who had closed herself off. Megan was the one who had panicked. I was doing everything I could to make our weekend special, wasn't I?

"Let's just watch a movie," I said through practically gritted teeth. And so we did, half-heartedly. The movie was about a girl falling in love with a traditional bull riding teenager in some part of Spain. The guy was young and handsome, the stereotype of a romantic hero. I couldn't help shake the feeling he was probably more Megan's type than me.

Maybe that's why she chose to watch it. Despite 80% of it consisting of her being sat on her phone. It was a petty train of thought to hold onto, but it felt impossible to shake.

The girl in the movie was afraid that an accident in the ring would take his life one day soon. It was a generic movie at best, but there were few better ways to pass the time between dinner and bed. The movie ended, and we found our way back to the bedroom. Megan took her medication as I immediately turned the light out. We lay in the tense darkness. I could feel it heavy in my throat.

"What's the matter Lucas?" I could feel her lying on her side next to me, her palms between her head and pillow.

As soon as Megan opened her mouth, I could no longer contain myself.

17

"What do you think the matter is?" I snapped, clearly taking Megan by surprise.

Taking myself by surprise. The room became deathly silent. A cold kind of silence. No crackling fire, soft music or movie faintly filling the background. Just two people. Breathing. Thinking.

The pressure inside me was building.

"I'm sorry. I've just been stressed out and..." she said.

"It doesn't matter, Megan. We're both tired. Let's just go to sleep."

"I won't sleep feeling like this."

"Can we try to go to sleep? Please?"

"Talk to me."

I took a long, deep breath. Inhale. Exhale. I felt my body deflating into the bed. My mind was conflicted.

One part was zen. Peaceful. Calm. This part understood the situation. There was clarity. It was late. The day had been rough. Emotions had been running high. Just leave it. There's nothing to gain.

The other part said fuck it. This had been a long time coming.

"Okay. Let's go." I sat up and turned the bedside lamp back on. "I'm sick of putting in what feels like 110% and getting nothing back. Don't get me wrong, I love that you booked this place. You drove us here and organised everything, but it feels so unmatched when it comes to you and me." I was lightly taking a moment to choose my words.

"I can't help but feel neglected," I continued. "From waking up and wanting a morning cuddle, playing in the supermarket, the shit car ride here, and whatever the fuck that was in the living room. What is this? You've been miserable all day."

It was harsh and aggressive, but it had been building up all day. It had to come out eventually. The bubble had popped.

"I hate that I make you feel that way. I just can't seem to get out of my head. I don't know what's wrong with me. I can't bring myself to do anything. I'm trying. I'm really trying."

"I know." I sighed. "Like this morning. I know you're the sort of person who wants to get things done, like when it comes to packing and that, and you want everything to be in order because then you can fully concentrate on us, but I don't know... It just grates on me. How hard is it to just want a kiss while I'm cooking or a cuddle while we're watching the movie? You just sat on your fucking phone while I did everything. You didn't even offer to help. I thought this was supposed to be an 'us' weekend. Not me catering for you and then just sitting in silence the whole time. I thought this was supposed to be a chance for us to move forward. It feels like you're living in the past."

"What does that mean?"

"Look. The whole thing with Matthew. It's whatever. It's done. I want to accept you as you are and not hold onto anything that's happened. We all make mistakes and do things wrong. I'm trying to remember that, and I know it takes time, but for fuck sake, can't we just be normal and be us? Remember us from a few months ago? Where has that us gone? Why is everything just feel so sensitive and heavy all the fucking time? It's driving me mad."

"I don't know. I'm just being me, at least I think I am. I don't really think about it. I guess being affectionate doesn't come naturally to me. At least not right now. I've told you, I don't know where I am right now. I'm sorry."

"But in the supermarket, it's like you don't just say 'hey, I'm busy doing this' in a playful way. I go to kiss you and you physically turn away. It's like I repulse you. That's how you make me feel. It's how I think of myself. Everything you do and everything that happens between us is like a giant fucking sign from the universe telling me you don't want to be with me." I sighed and took another deep breath, straightening my back against the headboard.

Megan sat up with me while biting her fingernails. There were a few moments of silence before I was convinced Megan wouldn't say anything, so I continued.

"Put it this way. You told me you believed in this fairy-tale kind of love where everything was perfect. You said you loved showing people how affectionate you could be, showering people with love, and having all these grand plans for your relationships. You want a big happy family. I'm not saying that we're going to have a family or whatever, I'm not saying that, but you get my point, right? You have this idea of who you want to be and this beautiful life, but it's like you don't understand it takes effort to make that happen. You actually have to do stuff. Sitting in silence the whole evening, being glued to your phone for a whole movie, or running off because a hand job didn't go the way you thought it would is pretty much as far away from that as you can get."

Silence. Megan stared into the duvet.

"I fell in love with that part of you," I said, "but I don't know where it is. I know this is, Jesus, the second time we've met, but I've never seen that side of you. Do you not feel that way towards me? If you don't, then maybe it would be best just to admit it so we can move on from it."

"No, I do. I do feel it, I just...," Megan paused. The silence grew again. "I always thought that I was always the affectionate one in a relationship, but I didn't realise there was a way of being more affectionate if that makes sense? I don't know. I feel like I'm a fraction as affectionate as you are."

"Jesus. I dread to think what your exes were like then if you were the affectionate one. Then again, one of them is cheating on his wife with you, so he's clearly scum," I said, instantly regretting my voice's aggressive.

My guiding voice came in for a moment. Why are you taking the conversation here? The voice was pushed out by emotion. Megan said nothing.

"I'm sorry, I know that was a shitty thing to say. I just feel needy and lost and I'm sorry. I'm just feeling really intense right now, and so frustrated. I wanted this to be this amazing weekend. Obviously you did too. There's just nothing happening. I don't feel anything. I mean, what the fuck happened in front of the fire earlier?"

"I don't know."

"I mean, I don't go down on you or do anything because I want something back. It's not like a fucking trade agreement or something, but to get up and just leave without saying anything?"

"You know it's not like that, Lucas. I don't know.

You had made everything so nice and then you were going down and I thought I wouldn't be able to make it as nice for you and I just freaked out. I thought you'd be upset with me because I didn't do anything back and I just had to get out. I can't deal with confrontation. Not right now."

"I get it but damn. Can you not see that walking off without saying anything is possibly the worst thing you can do?"

"I guess." Megan took a breath. "Can I ask you something?"

"Sure."

"If you love this romantic and loving side of me, but you've never seen it, then how can you say you love it?"

That lingered. I thought for a moment. It was hard to think of a straightforward answer. There were too many emotions passing through me. I knew what I wanted to say, but it felt impossible to think straight and organise it into a sentence.

"Because," I said, choosing my words carefully, "when we were getting to know each other, this is the way you painted yourself to be when in a relationship. There are not many people that have traditional values and such a wholesome outlook on life like you do, and I love it. Not that I've met, at least. So many girls I've known, whether being with them or as friends, just love getting caught up in drama and stuff like that. You're not like that. You're different. Your view on everything is different."

"But I'm not what you want either. Lucas. Be honest. You don't want to be with me. I feel hated. I can fucking feel it. It's all I feel. I never feel like I'm good enough. Ever. I can't live up to this standard you have of this affectionate person. I look at your face now and you're looking at me with such resent..."

Megan trailed off, visibly holding back tears. I realised I hadn't looked at her properly the whole time we talked. Seeing her like this made me feel so incredibly guilty. I shouldn't have been so irritated and spiteful. She was shutting down, closing herself off, barriers raising. I tried to pull it around.

Catching her eye, I cracked a half-smile.

"I'm sorry. You know I don't hate you. I think I just had this idea of this being a romantic weekend and we have this place to ourselves and I just wanted to be nice and connected with each other, you know? I had such high expectations that raised the bar too high. I don't mean it like that. It doesn't matter if you don't have the energy to be hyper or to show affection. You said you're going through a lot of stress. I should have been more accepting of that. From this morning onwards."

Megan nodded slowly. She slowed her voice right down.

"I thought for most of my life I was the affectionate one. Me and you being together has completely changed how I see myself. Like completely. I just have no idea who I am. I love being with you, but I also really love my own space. That's something I've never really thought about before."

Megan looked at me. I tried comforting her with my eyes, expressing it was okay to open up and carry on. But who knows what she saw. We can't know how others see us. It's what makes relationships so hard. Then again, would I even want to know what she saw? Could I bear it?

"I remember," she said slowly, "I already shared my fairy-tale type of love. I always believed I would get married to the first guy I dated when I was younger and in school, like 14 or 15. It was my first relationship. I told him that's how I felt and that I wanted to put the work in and be with him forever, and he just laughed at me. He called me immature for even thinking that kind of love existed. 'You really need a reality check', he said. That was the first time I ever told anyone how I felt, and it hurt so much. Now, I just don't know what I think. Now my whole vision of what I wanted has been blown out of the water, so where does that leave me?"

"I don't want you to force yourself to be someone you're not. This whole evening; don't worry about it. It's just me. I need to drop these expectations and just focus on being right here in reality. I'm sorry."

I pushed myself back down into bed, facing Megan, placing a hand on her leg. Without thinking, I started tracing circles on her skin with my fingertips. She pushed herself down, mirroring my position.

"It's hard, though," she said, her arms tangled in front of her chest. "I want to be like that. I want to be affectionate and loving. I just don't know how. I want to feel this overflow of emotions so it explodes out of me and I want to share that with you. I want to feel like that with you and towards my whole life. I want to feel passion. I want to feel something. I just don't have it. I don't have the energy to be like that."

"I don't know if it works like that. Have you ever felt like that before?"

Megan thought for a moment, nibbling the nail of her middle finger, glancing down to check her progress every few seconds.

"I don't think so."

"I think loving someone is a conscious effort. You've got to consciously look for the opportunities to put the effort in. I know I can seem needy and pushy at times, but I don't know, I guess it just comes naturally for me to want to be close with you. I know it can be a bit much sometimes though. I know I overcompensate from time to time as well."

"What do you mean?"

"Like, if I show you affection and get nothing back or feel blanked or ignored or neglected or whatever, I sometimes show more affection to try harder to get it back from you. I know that's wrong, basically like a trade agreement after all, but it's so unconscious. I know I shouldn't be so pushy, but I only ever see it in hindsight. I know this is how I come across as needy, and I know it pushes you away more. Like, maybe I tried too hard in the supermarket."

"I love getting affection from you Lucas. You're always so kind and caring. You always do things that make me smile. Your cuddles are so warm in the morning. Your wake-up texts are always so nice and they really help get me through the day, but my emotions are just so much. It's so easy to go along with the dark thoughts. I get so tangled up in them and it just leaves me feeling so scared and anxious all the time. Those feelings are so far away from, well, love."

Megan went to open her mouth, but no more words came out. I watched her eyes glaze over as she stared blankly over my shoulder and onto the wall behind me. I glimpsed the clock on the bedside table behind her.

It was 2am. Megan's Quetiapine had a sleeping effect that would have long taken effect at this point and it was far too late to carry on any kind of conversation.

18

Minutes passed.

I watched as Megan, almost in slow motion, rested her head back down on the bed, eyes closed. She looked peaceful, an image shattered by the single tear that rolled out of the corner of her eye and sunk into the pillow.

At that moment, she broke.

Abruptly, she covered her face with her hands and erupted into violent sobs.

"Oh Lucas, I'm so sorry. I've completely ruined this weekend. I feel so guilty. Why can't I just be okay? What the fuck is wrong with me?"

Whatever Megan said next was distorted by her cries. The tears poured. I reached out, putting a hand to her face to wipe some tears away. I tried to get closer to wrap my arms around her, but she was shaking far too much, wrenching and curled over. I just wanted to help. I just wanted to be close to her. I just wanted to make everything okay.

"I'm sorry. I didn't mean to upset you. You haven't ruined anything. Trust me. We're just working things out. We're still getting to know each other and this is just part of the process. I just want to do what makes you feel better. Is it us? Are we the problem that's making you feel sad?"

Megan looked me dead in the eyes before crying harder than ever before. She stopped, suddenly plunging the room back into the deadly silence without warning. The shift was surreal. She sat up again and stared hard into the wall at the end of the bed.

"Hey, come here. Lay back down," I said, rubbing her back softly with one hand. "You'll be asleep soon. We can talk about it all in the morning when we're feeling more awake."

I tried to lay her down and hold her. She said nothing, but instead her head collapsed into her hands. I ran my fingertips over her back, trying to think of something to say that wouldn't be the wrong thing. It was Megan who broke the tension, speaking into her lap.

"I don't want to make you unhappy, Lucas. I don't want to make you sad. I can't do that. I couldn't live with myself if I hurt you more than I have already. Fuck, I'm such a bitch."

"You're not a bitch" Before I could say anything else, Megan pulled her head out of her hands and began scratching her arm, dragging her nails down over the skin of her wrists. The first few scratches left white lines. The fourth made the skin red, and in the places where she had been biting her nails and had left sharp leftovers, she drew blood.

"Megan, stop. It's okay. Everything's okay. I promise. We can talk about this all another day. It's been a bit of a heavy and stressful day today, what with Lisa's email and all the driving. We're both just overtired and need a good sleep. Trust me. Everything's fine."

I reached out and gently tried to stop her hands from moving, but she kept going, getting more aggressive with every scratch.

"I hate myself. I can't live with myself." She scratched again, and this time I grabbed her wrist abruptly to stop her from pushing further into her skin. She still refused to look anywhere but into the nothingness ahead of her.

"Lucas." She stopped and looked me dead in the eyes. I hadn't been able to look at her properly, but she was gone. Her pupils were like black holes, void of life, filled with emptiness. I saw nothing but darkness.

"How sharp are the knives in the kitchen?"

The words lingered. A sickness rippled throughout my body. I remembered the knives in the knife rack well. A collection of all different sizes and shapes for all sorts of cutting purposes. I'm not a chef, so I didn't really know what all of them were used for, but the one thing I do know is that every single one was razor-sharp. Almost as if they had been sharpened for our arrival.

"Actually not sharp at all", I lied through my teeth. "I was quite surprised with how blunt they were, considering all the pots and pans are good. Must be for if children stay here."

I blew it at the end because there was no chance children stayed in that romantic cottage for two, but I know Megan wasn't thinking straight, so it seemed to pass her by. Quickly, I changed the subject.

"Hey, how about we go for a shower? That could be really grounding. Just take our minds off things. Yeah? I think we just need to get out of the room. Maybe a cold shower would be best?" I needed one. I felt sick.

"I'm not having a fucking cold shower."

"Okay, we can have a hot shower, although I think cold showers are supposed to be really good for clarity."

"I will literally murder you if you come near me with cold water." I knew Megan was joking, although a part of me flinched just in case. What if Megan was gone and some dark part of her consciousness had taken over completely? I tried to suss her out but couldn't tell. I looked her up and down. She looked like Megan, sounded like her. She still smelled like the shampoo and shower gel from earlier, only now mingled with salty tears. Maybe I was just feeding off her anxieties. And it was late. I was tired.

"Okay. Warm slash hot shower then. Please? Do it for me?" I regretted my choice of language, but it appeared to go unnoticed.

It took some convincing, but finally Megan agreed to come with me. Dazed and confused, senses heightened by anxiety and spaced out by medicine, she let me undress her before sitting in the shower tray together. I wrapped my arm around her, and she nestled into the space of my shoulder where her head fit perfectly.

I played with the falling water with my free hand while we sat. I was only once tempted to make the water cold, but Megan smiled and hit me.

After we started to get cold and tinkered with the sauna but failed at getting it to work, I wrapped Megan in a towel, dried her off and dressed her in her pyjamas. She was pretty out of it by the time I walked her back to bed before going back into the bathroom to finish drying and dressing myself to then join her.

I turned the light off in bed and wrapped my arms around her, stroking her skin softly with my fingers.

"It's okay," I said in the most comforting voice I could muster, "We're both tired. Let's just get some sleep and have a good day tomorrow."

Megan was asleep within minutes of putting her head down. My mind raced. What if this weekend is it? The last weekend we spent together.

There's no way we could stay together if all we were doing was making each other miserable, especially if it's going to end up with scenes like that and her wanting to hurt herself. Imaginary thoughts of Megan cutting herself and ending up in hospital plagued me.

Visions of me standing next to a hospital bed, the pings of heartbeat machines and monitors beeping around me. Her parents stand opposite. We look down as Megan is motionless, pipes and tubes coming out of her body from all angles, sedatives keeping her in place. I glance down at the bandage on her arm, a cotton wrap soaked in blood, and wince yet remain unable to take my eyes off it.

I shuddered back to the reality of the cottage and forced myself to stay awake until gone five in the morning in case she needed me. I couldn't sleep. My mind raced with the images of potential futures. Once I was sure Megan was asleep, I crept up and back into the kitchen to get a glass of water. I dazed at the low, fading embers in the tray of the wood burner. Glowing ashes soon to shine their last light.

A cigarette outside the back door would be perfect right about now. I then moved for a minute on the island counter and stared into the darkness before convincing myself that sleeping in bed, not in the lounge, was the best idea.

Before heading back to the bedroom, I placed the knife rack under the kitchen sink.

19

We drove back from the cottage Sunday afternoon and I took the train back to London early on Monday morning.

While the emotions of the weekend still plagued me, like an insanely continuous echo fading out gradually with every cycle, life near-enough returned to normal not long after. The good kind of normal. Me and Megan texted each other all day and video called most nights until we fell asleep.

We read books, played games, and streamed movies together, taking a few minutes at the start to make sure our films were lined up and playing them from the same place at the same time.

Megan's university work was still as stressful as ever, and a few times we would talk about emotions and how tense life was. She cut herself on two occasions. At least two that I knew of. Not deep, each instance just a single line down her arm. Once was while we video called, although I didn't see it happen graphically.

I asked her several times if she was planning on seeing someone to talk about it all to a therapist or counsellor. She said she had tried in the past, but they never seemed to help. We didn't see each other again until two months later. It was the middle of August by then; the peak of summer.

While I had planned to take the train up to Scotland as I had last time, we decided the night before that we'd prefer to meet halfway. It had been a trying month for both of us and we agreed it would be best to enjoy a nice change of scenery, if only for a day.

We just needed a little escape from the mundanity of our everyday lives, so we settled on meeting in Blackpool.

Sure, it wasn't the most romantic of places and was a little out of the way for both of us, but neither of us had visited before, and it is supposedly a highlight of the UK.

However, neither of us could remember, nor could figure out, why. It had the tower and the pier, so we agreed that the trip would be a success as long as we saw those.

We took early trains and met on parallel platforms at Blackpool station. Seeing her for the first time after the steady month we'd had was heartwarming.

Images flickered across my mind of meeting at

King's Cross and the awkwardness we had felt. It's funny to look back on. I remember it as a positive time. Rose-tinted? Perhaps. Kind of cute and romantic. Pre-date jitters and all that.

Even then, months after meeting, we still felt that same shudder of nerves, but we were so much more comfortable. We were connected. We were in each other's lives.

We drifted through the town and checked into a hotel to drop our bags off. It was 11am by the time we hit the streets in search of breakfast and adventure. Hand in hand, we roamed the seafront, alternating between excessive arm swinging and trying to squeeze both our hands inside my jacket pocket.

Despite being a toasty 24 degrees, hot for a British morning, Megan still said the sea air was making her hands cold. On the hunt for a remedy, we found a coffee shop near the tower and sat down for something to eat.

While waiting for food, I fabricated a game where I would pick one of the pieces of student art covering the walls of the café and ask Megan what that piece meant to her. Megan had no interest in art, and since many of the pieces were abstract messes with no real shape or form, she didn't really have much opinion about any of them.

"It doesn't matter what you say," I said, "It's about what you get from it personally. Like what does it make you think of, or how does it make you feel?"

Perhaps what I thought was a game was annoying for Megan. Perhaps I needled her.

I wonder, now, slightly older, slightly wiser, if I read Megan wrong a lot of the time. Questions that will never have answers.

"I don't know," she said, staring at the canvas littered with black and white blobs that looked like a giant paintbrush had just flicked paint across the board before it was considered complete. Truth be told, I didn't get it either.

"It makes me think of... a mess."

"Yeah, that is pretty messy. What about that one?" I said, nodding towards a standard drawing of a cow, but a cow that had been coloured in the most rainbow way possible.

It's colourful."

"Oh, good eyes Picasso. Wait, you've heard of Picasso, right?" Megan said nothing, and I smiled as the waitress came over and placed our sandwiches and coffee down on the table. Megan hated sandwiches, so I don't know why she ordered one.

She had a habit of panic ordering under pressure and never really taking the time to choose what she really wanted.

"Thank you," I nodded at the waitress. "Oh, come on. You must have at least heard the name?"

"I told you, I'm not into that kind of stuff. I don't really like culture stuff; you know, music or whatever. Just give me a mountain to walk up or a forest to walk through and I'll be happy."

"So, why say you wanted to meet in Blackpool when we could have just gone somewhere wild and you'd have been happy? I mean, the Peak District is only up the road. We could have just got a tent to go and stay in the woods somewhere? Fuck spending all the money on a hotel."

We both fell silent. Megan stared at me with one of the cheekiest grins I had seen in a long time. Her face confessed the idea tempted her.

"I mean, we could, right?" she asked. I thought for a moment. We had already paid for the hotel and had bags with us. I was comfortable with what we were doing now, but at the same time, I hadn't done anything spontaneous in a long time. And who knows, maybe it could be fun. The adventure was sealed with a smile.

We finished our food and drinks, Megan barely touching her sandwiches, and spent some time scrolling around on her Maps app to find a decent place in the Peak District that drew our gaze.

Neither of us fancied a traditional camping site but would instead just pick some remote place in the middle of nowhere with nobody else around. Sod's law we'd end up with a camping site next to a family with crying children or teenagers getting drunk.

Quiet. Out of the way. In our bubble. Just how we liked it.

We settled on a rather remote lake that had a single

lovely picture someone had uploaded several years ago, and the fact it was close to a mountain clearly excited Megan. We decided to go and left. It felt decisive. Excited.

We bought a cheap tent from a local camping store with some food supplies from the supermarket and Googled a car rental place up the northern end of the seafront. Everything was organised by one in the afternoon, and we were ready to rock and roll. We checked out of the hotel room and chucked our bags in the back of the car while taking one last walk down the seafront towards the tower.

"I mean, we've at least got to get a picture of the tower while we're here. What are the chances we'll never come back here again?" I said, fiddling with the camera app on my phone.

"We?"

"I mean, either of us. I don't think I will. Not much going on, is there? Want to get in?"

"No," said Megan, "I don't like having my photo taken."

"Oh, come on. I won't put it on Instagram or anything. Come on, you look beautiful. Let's take a selfie."

Megan reluctantly moved close to me and I put my arm around her. With her free arm, she pulled her jumper, the light green one, up over her face to her nose and buried her head into my neck, so only the right side of her face and right eye showed.

I smiled and hit the button a load of times, taking a burst of photos, moving the camera every time to try and get a better angle of the tower behind our heads. Megan laughed a little as I clearly had no idea what I was doing photography-wise, but she seemed pretty amused by my attempts.

The photos still move something in me whenever I scroll past them briefly on my phone.

"I always feel really stupid taking a selfie. This is why I don't take them. It just feels uncomfortable, you know?" I said.

"Me neither. I think they're pretentious," said Megan in a teasing voice.

"Oi. Forgive me for wanting to remember our time in Blackpool. Don't you want a copy?" "Put them in our Dropbox folder?"

"Sure, I'll do it when I get home. Shall we go then?"

We walked back to the car hand-in-hand and set off out of the city. We never discussed who would be driving, but I knew Megan got a little anxious when it came to driving in new places, especially in a different car to her own, so we silently agreed I'd take the wheel.

After setting up a Google Maps route to a dropped pin in some woods near a lake in the general Peak District area, Megan connected her phone to the radio and searched through her playlists.

We settled on Avril Lavigne and other nostalgic classics, and after the few quiet miles it took to get out of the city, we became increasingly confident with our

146

first mumbled singing, eventually until we were singing 'I'm with You' at the top of our voices.

Much to Megan's embarrassment, I got carried away and wound down the windows to sing to the people we drove past or in other cars whenever we reached a set of traffic lights or a roundabout.

Our journey took us further and further into the middle of nowhere, and after lots of joking that this kind of area would be the perfect place to murder and bury someone, we parked up in a small car park practically hidden off the tree-lined road. I scoped the place out.

A footpath stemmed from the main car park and ran into the woods and then up the side of a large hill on the other side of the car park. It looked as though people rarely came here since the car parking spaces were overgrown with weeds, and the picnic benches near a small noticeboard that only housed faded posters seemed to be rotting and moulding in places.

"Huh. Is there such a thing as abandoned Peak District car parks?" I asked. Megan was too busy looking up into the canopy above the car park to answer. Even from here, I could see her face was glowing, her smile beaming.

The huge, new-looking metal barrier that closed off what I would guess to be a Forestry Commission track and stopped people from driving down it was the only sign of modern life.

Fortunately, there was no car park ticket machine or

pay and display sign, especially since neither of us had any cash. We hauled our stuff out of the car and glossed over Google Maps. There was no obvious path to get to our chosen lake, which was supposedly located on the right side of the hill, but still seemed miles away.

"Which way do you reckon we should go?" Megan asked.

"That's completely up to you, Captain. I'll be your humble, er, matey."

"Yeah. My glorified bag carrier. I'll lead then."

Megan set off ahead cross country into the forest on a beeline directly for where she thought the lake would be. We'd come this far. We just had to commit. Walking through the woods was a beautiful experience.

It was roughly half four by the time the car park slipped out of view behind us, and the golden early-evening sunlight was beaming through the trees, creating pillars of light that we detoured to pass through whenever one was just within walking distance, guiding us like beacons along our overgrown trail.

The beams were like pillars in a church -- and the forest is a church to many.

Maybe it was to Megan.

The only sounds came from the birds taking off overhead at our arrival and the sound of occasional gusts of wind through the leaves. Every now and then,

I would start mumbling a bit of Avril Lavigne or Natasha Bedingfield, suddenly shouting a line of the chorus randomly. Megan jumped suddenly every time. So did the flocks of birds erupting above us.

We walked side by side where possible, but I took the lead on some parts of the trail, whenever a branch needed to be held up or back or whenever the undergrowth became so thick it needed pushing down. Megan watched me, phone with the map app open in one hand, the tent bag in the other, as I ploughed through the forest.

Occasionally, I turned back to look at her, just checking she was okay and that I wasn't going to hit her with a pushed-out branch and smiled. Although we had been dating six months or so, Megan told me a few weeks later over one of our nightly video calls that this trip was the first time she really felt any intense feelings for me.

I like to think these forested moments in this kind of church were the moments where she felt it.

She said she watched me pushing through the trees as visions of marrying me flashed across her mind or me standing next to her as she rested in a hospital bed holding our child. She imagined a cottage in the middle of nowhere with a little, slightly-fallen cobblestone wall and horses in the neighbouring paddock. She saw me driving a ride-on lawnmower across the back garden, children chasing up and down behind me.

She said that she had asked herself whether this was what falling in love felt like.

20

An hour passed.

Early evening had cooled the day. The sky was still a brilliant clear blue with red and pink clouds deepening their shades by the minute. We emerged from a break in the trees, and there it was; the glorious turquoise lake stretched out in front of us about half a mile across.

It was much smaller than we thought it would be from the scale of the map, but there didn't seem to be anywhere significant close by, nor any signs that people came here, apart from the pheasant feeders set up on the other side of the water. The only sound came from the light wind passing through the trees, the calls of distant birds, and crickets hiding nearby in the long grass that quietened themselves as we got near.

"Wow, it's beautiful here. It's so calm," I said as I dropped down onto the shorter grass around the banks of the lake and sat to take it all in. Megan sat down gently next to me and was clearly finding it hard to hide the smile her face kept making.

"What's up with you? I asked, taking the rucksack off and kissed her on the cheek.

"Nothing," said Megan, still smiling. "I'm just happy."

We kissed, and then Megan rested her head on my shoulder to gaze out across the lake together. The wind had mostly stopped, making everything seem incredibly still and peaceful. We were free in that moment. A surreal reality.

I imagined that some people were arguing somewhere in the world right now. Some people were breaking up. Some people held their baby for the first time, and others had their first kiss.

But we were just here, being us, inside our bubble, looking out at the world in front of us. When a breeze blew through, we watched the ripples rise up from the left side of the lake and pass all the way across before crashing into the parallel bank.

There was nothing we needed to do. Nowhere else we wanted to be.

We sat for a solid hour just enjoying the passing of moments before I suggested we set the tent up and get everything sorted. After struggling with the positions for the poles and trying to find a bit of ground that was soft enough to stick the pegs in, the tent was set up with no issues. Since we didn't have sleeping bags, we emptied our bags of clothes and spread them out over the groundsheet of the tent. There weren't many, but it would do.

We opened and lit our disposable barbecue to heat it up and spent a couple of minutes looking over our food, making sure the sausages we had brought were still okay to eat after being in the hot car for so long.

We both shrugged and decided we didn't really care. We took turns rolling the sausages over on the gauze and splitting the buns. We shimmied down the bank to the water's edge to find good stones for skimming in between turns.

There weren't any ideal flat pebbles, so we just tried to find the biggest rocks possible, throwing them as far and as hard as possible to see who could make the biggest splash.

We laughed, chatted, and messed around for hours as the sun sank below the tree line before disappearing below the horizon, causing the sky to explode into a scene of gorgeous reds and oranges. While staring at clouds and watching them float across the sky, we erupted into a tickle fight out of nowhere that ended with me rolling onto Megan, pinning her down by her legs.

She forfeited with kisses but claimed she would never fully surrender. I asked her one more time to give herself up. She refused, broke free and tickled me back so hard I rolled off her and down the bank, stopping only centimetres from the water's edge. We fed each other hotdogs and ate the salad with our hands before chilling in the porch of the tent until it got dark enough that we couldn't see anything.

There was no artificial light for miles around, not like there was in the city. I finally made sure the barbecue was out before getting into the tent, closing up the bug netting flap behind me.

Last but most importantly, I pulled a book out of my bag to read as Megan's bedtime story. She'd taken her pill and fell asleep before the end of the first page, so I read a chapter to myself, turned out the light, kissed her goodnight on the forehead, and fell asleep minutes later.

We slept soundly, like animals hibernating in our den.

21

It was a sudden bang in the near-distance that woke us the following morning.

A bang followed by the rustling of the bushes and long grass near the head end of our tent. I was just about conscious, stirring sleepily while Megan was quickly wide awake and sat bolt upright, straining to make out the sound. The rustling continued. I fully woke to Megan jabbing me in the ribs.

"It's probably just an animal, a muntjac or something. Don't worry about it," I tried to lie down again, content with my own excuses. The tent was the same muggy heat that comes after every night I've ever spent in a tent. Megan was convinced otherwise as the sound grew closer. The tightening grip of her hand on my arm confirmed her fear.

"Good morning," a booming man's voice called out

from just outside the tent. The rustling stopped. A silhouette appeared on the fabric of the tent.

Megan panicked. The heat that had built up inside the tent made it much more oppressive. It was so stuffy I could hear she was having trouble breathing. I sat up, pulled off my now-soggy, sweat-drenched t-shirt, and unzipped the bug netting at the front.

"Morning. How are you?" I said, climbing out of the tent and stretching my arms outwards. The man was clearly a farmer from the local area, judging by how he dressed. Shit. I knew what was coming.

Fortunately, we had cleared up any rubbish from the food before and put all the rubbish into a bag inside the tent, I thought to myself. Only the disposable BBQ tin, which had been left to cool by the water, was outside.

"I'm terrific, thank you," the man replied. "Can I ask you a question?"

"Sure, is everything okay?" I replied, leaning back inside the tent to grab the water bottle by the entrance. Megan pulled my t-shirt close to her and held it tightly in her hands in front of her chest.

"Do you have permission to be here?" the man asked.

"Er, no. From the Peak District Commission?"

"No, from the landowner, you fuck." I stepped back a single step from the aggression.

"No, we don't," I said. I tried to remain completely calm but was not awake enough for this kind of confrontation. My blood started to heat. Skin prickled.

"You know this is my land? How dare you think you can just swan over here and camp up. What gives you the right? How about I just grab a tent and come and sleep in your back garden? Is that okay?"

"I mean, I wouldn't really..."

"Don't you get smart with me, boy," The man's temper rapidly became more intense by the second.

"We're very sorry, Sir. We'll leave right now. We won't leave any litter or anything. We can assure you it won't happen again."

"Too fucking right it won't. What's your name? Who else have you got here?" The man moved around to the front of the tent and bent down to look inside. Megan recoiled a little as his head peered in. Megan was terrified, and she made no attempt to hide it, pulling the t-shirt up to her face quickly. She looked as though she couldn't move.

"I see," the man said, standing back upright to address me. "So, you just thought you'd come out here to fuck?"

"No. Just hiking. As I said, we're ever so sorry. We didn't realise this was private land. We were hiking yesterday and lost track of time, and it got dark, so we thought we would stay. No harm intended."

"Oh yeah, because there's a campsite around here, isn't there? You just happened to bring your tent and sleeping bags along, hey?"

"No. That doesn't even make sense. Look, we didn't

know. We're not from around here." I didn't bother correcting him by saying we didn't have sleeping bags.

"I say again, and for the last time. What's your name?"

"You don't need to know that. We're just going to pack our stuff and go." I looked over at Megan and mouthed the word "pack". Megan didn't see what I said.

Even though I saw her with a glance, she seemed to be fighting off a panic attack. Yet, she must have felt what I meant or noticed me mentioning towards her as she began putting everything back into bags. The man stepped right up to my face, so I could smell the musky scent of old cigarettes on his breath, mixed sourly with a morning coffee. Was that alcohol as well?

"If you don't tell me your name, I will call the police and have you both prosecuted for trespassing."

"Then go and call the police. Honestly, I think I'd much rather speak with them. Look, we're just going to go. No problems, right?" I said, unflinching and not stepping back from the man.

This only seems to enrage the man further, leading him to push himself closer to me without physically moving. I could sense how much tension his body held. My fist balled around the car keys in my pocket.

While we were only silent for a second, bar from the sound of the wind and the birds waking up, it felt like several minutes. An image flickered across the front of my mind. Stabbing the guy in the neck with the long part of the car key. I would never, but if I had to, in self-defence. Maybe? My instinct was running through potential outcomes, prepping for the eventuality.

"Look, you little shit," he said, jamming a finger up, stopping just millimetres from my face. "I don't know how you got here or who the fuck you think you are thinking you can come onto private property like this, but if you and your bitch girlfriend here don't leave now, I'm calling the police. You have twenty minutes. If I come back here and you're not gone, there'll be hell to pay."

I took a deep inhale.

The image of punching this guy or pushing him back so he fell into the lake, crossed my mind. I was immensely satisfied by the idea of it but decided to bite my tongue and not say anything. I was conflicted between getting out as fast as possible and avenging the 'little bitch' remark, but I didn't want to scare Megan even more than I knew she was already.

"Fine."

The man looked at me, then to Megan, and back to me again before suddenly storming back around the lake's edge towards the pheasant feeders. There, his truck was parked, backed up to the feeder. As soon as he was a few metres away, we started packing everything up as quickly as possible, occasionally looking over to see what the man was.

We didn't speak. I smiled in Megan's direction once, but she was solely focused on stuffing clothes into bags as quickly as possible.

Once we had pulled everything out of the tent, I pulled it down and tried to squeeze everything into the tent bag. This was proving a struggle without taking time to fold everything correctly, so we instead used the tent's guide ropes to knot everything in place tightly.

"What a fucking dick," said I as we finished folding the tent down, holding the bundle of messy fabric together with the weight of my knee. "Why does he have to be so aggressive?"

"Don't worry. Let's just leave, okay?"

"Are you okay?" "Yeah. I'm just a little shaky."

"Don't worry, let's just go now."

"Sure." I swung the rucksack onto my shoulder and took the tent bag in the other hand, half of the folded bits immediately coming loose and now hanging outside my makeshift guide rope knot. Megan took her bag and the rubbish bag, making sure to take the disposable barbecue and stood with seemingly absolutely no idea in which direction we should be heading.

Stress and anger were the greatest feelings above all else. I couldn't think straight. Images of punching the guy or stabbing him with the car key mixed with adrenaline surged through my body.

I would never do it, but the idea felt so satisfying. I tried to take charge of our little expedition and headed towards the woods, following the trodden grass from the day before. I couldn't decide.

"Do you know where we're going?" I swung around to ask Megan. She was looking sheepishly at the floor. I could tell by her expression she was on mental lockdown.

"It's okay. Nothing bad has happened."

I took her by the hand and pulled her in the direction I thought we were heading. I didn't look back until we reached the edge of the trees. The man seemed to be on the phone.

"Oi," I called out at the top of my voice before we crossed back the tree line. "Fuck you, cunt."

I added an extra sneer to the final word, venting every milligram of hatred and anger I felt towards him in that moment. What a release!

"No, stop!" Megan said quietly, as though the man would be able to hear our normal voices. Her hand touched my arm.

"Why? He is. He's completely ruined what was otherwise such a perfect night. How can he speak to two human beings in such an aggressive, disgusting way?"

The adrenaline started to wear off, and I was coming to my senses. Okay, maybe it was unnecessary. It felt good, though. Megan said nothing and continued to look at the ground.

"I'm sorry. Come on."

I took her hand, and we darted off into the woods, following a deer-trodden down path in the undergrowth until we found what looked like the same path from the day before.

Neither of us spoke until we got back to the car. We threw our bags into the backseat, got in, and set off back down the road the way we came.

"Are you okay?" I said once we got a little way away from the car park.

"Can you put the postcode for the car place in?" I struggled to slip my phone out of my pocket between changing gears and handed it to Megan.

"Why did you shout at him?" "I don't know. I was angry at him. I mean, he was a cunt. He could have been nice about it."

"Yeah, but you shouldn't call people that. It's not nice." I went to reply several times but said nothing. Instead, we sat in stiff silence.

"Yeah, I know. I'm sorry." I finally managed, gritting my teeth as a police car drove past in the other direction with the lights flashing.

Neither of us spoke until a few miles later when it seemed the police car had not been dispatched for us. We hit the main road and followed it all the way back to Blackpool. Handing the car back was easy, although we sneakily left the tent and rubbish bag still in the backseats.

We then decided to walk along the beachfront in the sun, which seemed surprisingly quiet for a summer Sunday morning. We sat on a small wall with our feet drawing circles in the sand and looked up returning train times.

"I had a really nice time with you this weekend," I said, gazing out to the sea before smiling at Megan.

"Yeah. Me too. It was really nice. I just..."

"Just what?"

"I just don't think you should have spoken to the farmer like that. I saw so much anger and hate in your eyes. It scared me."

"It was only adrenaline. You know, being hyped up in the moment. Something like that. Really. It's nothing to worry about. Did you see how close he got to me? How could I not be defensive?"

"I don't like anger. It scares me. I've never seen you like that before. You feel like a stranger."

Those last five words stung like an acid blade stabbing into my heart. I desperately tried to turn things around.

"No, it's okay. Just a momentary outburst. It's good to vent like that sometimes. You don't need to be scared of anything. What's he going to do? Hit us? Doesn't matter if we're on private land. That would be assault. Probably wasn't even his land anyway. Probably just a slave to some rich guy."

"That's not the point. What if you get that angry at me?" I tried to think reasonably. It was a valid point, but nothing I could say could prove otherwise.

My mind remained racing desperately to change the images in Megan's head.

"It wasn't too bad. It was literally all just self-defence.

Let's say you get up in my face like that, saying what he said. Of course I'll act like it back. But it's all words and no action. Besides, it just makes the whole experience more memorable, you know? Remember the cuddles, kisses, reading, tickling, and chatting. It was really a perfect night."

"I thought you didn't believe in perfection?"

"Well, last night was close enough."

We smiled and kissed, then sat back in our chairs and faced forward. Something felt off. There was a stiffness to her lips, but it felt good to be moving forward. I regretted the anger but was sure Megan could let it go. I wasn't even angry.

Anyone would be in the same situation. I used to think how one event like that couldn't possibly taint the way someone saw you. Yet, in some ways, it was never the same afterwards. As we sat on the seafront, we had been together just coming up to 24 hours, but it seemed like we had been each other's company for weeks.

Our day-to-day lives, the university course, my job, our bills, friendship dramas, and plans for the year. All of it seemed so distant in this moment, as though it was all in other people's lives. Thinking back to that weekend, despite the drama, I remember how beautifully I felt towards Megan.

From walking through the woods to lying in the tent and forgetting the world in such a beautiful setting. Everything, from the weather to the stillness of the evening, seemed like a sign from the universe that us being together was the right thing to happen. It was meant to be.

But was it real life? Was I trying to convince myself everything was okay while only remembering the good?

While we sat on that wall together, we both sat alone. Crazy how we didn't even know each other existed just a year before. Now we were so ingrained in each other's lives. Integral parts. Essential parts.

In another year's time, we might not even think of each other anymore, and weekends like our time in the Peak District would be long forgotten bar the occasion photograph we may come across while scrolling through our phones or from the appearance of a fleeting memory.

The ripple of a stone tossed into a lake long ago.

22

It didn't last.

After returning home from Blackpool, Megan and I drifted and became distant. All-day texting sessions and night times filled with video calls, video games and bedtime stories had fizzled out without so much of a word from each other.

If asked to describe it all in one word, I'd choose natural. And if I was being honest, I was glad to have the space.

Without comment nor realisation, I started spending more time with Aaron and Amy. We watched movies, and I joined them for dinner after work. Their friends came round for a board game and drinks night. It was a nice change. For one, it felt as though I wasn't trapped in my obsessive thoughts. I could breathe and smile in a way where I really meant it. I could feel a kind of happiness behind my lips. I couldn't believe I hadn't joined them before.

I spent a week catching up with other friends who were dotted about the city. It was pretty fun, and many of my friends, some of whom I realised I hadn't really spoken to in two or three years now, had changed in many ways.

Some had worse drinking, drug, or money habits than when I previously saw them. Some had fled the scene and were starting to work on projects of their own. Others were settling down with their partners, buying first houses, and starting families. It was all incredibly eye-opening.

It felt as though some invisible walls had existed around me and held me in place. Stopped me from seeing the outside world and, in a sense, reality. All I'd been looking at was a tight and narrow box where I could see what was in front of me and a projection of my own echo-chambered thoughts.

These walls were falling down.

Beyond those barriers was an entirely new and beautiful world full of opportunities. It quickly dawned on me that something in my life desperately needed to change. For the first time in many years, I realised I was miserable.

While meeting Megan had seemed like an explosion of light into my life, I hadn't taken the time to think about why it was so grey in the first place. I noticed increasingly suicidal thoughts crossed my mind daily.

Not the idea of doing it. I can't say I ever would. Instead, it was a line of thinking rooted in fear. Fear of losing control to an all-consuming thought that would make me follow through. I wondered what it was like. My brain taunted me, curious as to what it would be like on the edge.

How far down you'd have to go to do it. These thoughts terrified me. Were they real? Did I really want that to happen, or was it just a part of me that wanted to die?

One night I lost myself playing video games.

After losing several games in a row, I'd become particularly 'toxic' in the in-game chat, calling people out for little mistakes and being somewhat abusive. The insults and aggressive comments flowed out of me so unconsciously. I wasn't thinking. When I went to log into the next game, a popup notified me my account had been banned for two weeks. No more games for now then. That moment was a lightning strike of reality. Who was I? What was I doing in my life?

Calling strangers on the internet 'useless fucks' because we'd lost a round of a game? I was channelling, projecting my misery, and so it dawned on me to make a change. I never thought I would be that guy, but there I was, and it was time to take a stance. I didn't know how yet, but the winds of change were starting to pick up pace. I needed to get out of London.

The night after being banned, Megan drifted back into my text messages. I tried to explain how I felt. God, did I try, yet I never felt anything but misunderstood and more determined for change after that conversation.

"I can't believe you got banned. You must have been horrible."

"Yeah, it was pretty bad. I don't know what came over me. Anyway, it's in the past, and I just want to move on."

"I think that's a good idea. And I'm sure you'll find something. You're a smart cookie."

"I hope so. I don't know what it was, but I just woke up in that moment and questioned everything. I don't want to be here, doing what I do now in five years' time. Hell, I don't want to be doing any of this in a week, so might as well make a change now, you know?"

"Yeah. I'm glad you feel that way though. You have seemed pretty down."

"Yeah, just stressed out."

I lost my train of thought staring out the window blankly while listening to Amy's laugh rise up through the floor at something on TV. I'd been blanking like that a lot recently. Not in a bad way. Just peacefully pausing to experience the world in that moment. I didn't want to have this conversation. I wanted to be laughing downstairs with them.

"Lucas?"

"Yeah?"

"Are you okay?"

"I literally just said I was stressed out. And tired. How was your day anyway?"

"Yeah, it was okay. Everyone is being so annoying. We have a new first-year starting next week, and I have to teach him to use the computers and stuff. I'm so busy as it is."

"Why don't you just say no? Surely it's not your job?"

"I already said I was going to do it."

"Then say no now?"

"No, I have to. I just. I don't know. It's so much."

"Megan. In the nicest way possible, listen to yourself. You're literally putting yourself in this situation. You just had to say no and you wouldn't have to do it. I don't know why they're asking you anyway. Surely it's Lisa's job or someone from the office?"

"I was actually quite excited about doing it and I thought you'd be more supportive. I thought it could be a nice new experience. Something new."

"You literally just said you were stressed and didn't want to do it?"

"I never said I didn't want to do it. I just said it was a lot and it was stressful. I do want to help people though. Remember I wanted to volunteer? This could be a good start. Small steps and all that."

"Then make your mind up. If you want to do it,

then be happy about doing it. Stop complaining about it. Fuck me, you keep doing this all the time."

"Doing what?"

"Complaining!"

Megan fell silent. I could feel my anger, those toxic notes, creeping back into my voice. Megan was going into her usual shutdown. I took a deep breath. Some part of me was fuming that she had, once again, made the conversation all about her. It always was. How did we always end up here?

Granted, I could feel my lack of patience. Everything was grating.

"I'm sorry. I'm just stressed and tired. I don't mean to sound angry. There's a lot on my mind and I'm just trying to process it all."

"Ah, I'm so annoyed."

"At what?"

"Myself. You sounded so hopeful and ready to change when we started talking, and now you're upset and angry at me. I can't do anything right."

"It's not that. I wanted to talk to you about wanting to do something big and make some big life change, and once again, we're talking about your problems. If you want to do something, do it. If you don't want to do something, don't do it. If you make a choice, don't come and complain to me about it. Can we please just be a bit more positive?"

"I'm sorry. I'm just struggling..." Something in her tone of voice tugged at a heart string.

"Don't be sorry. I know you are. Look, we've spoken about it already. Just take some time off. Regroup your thoughts. Find yourself again. I don't know. Just have a break from it all."

"I guess."

"I'm going to go to bed. I'm too tired for this conversation. Speak to you soon?"

"Yeah. Okay. Night."

"Wait."

"What?"

"Please don't just go off and be upset. We can sleep on this and feel better in the morning. You know?"

"Yup."

I wasn't about to get into a fight with her nor play at her pity party and try to make her feel better before going to sleep, yet some massive part of me was begging to make the situation a little brighter before hanging up the phone.

Thinking about it now, I'm a little ashamed of myself then. Younger Lucas unable to parse his own feelings, unable to help Megan with hers. So lost in emotion. So wrapped up in it all.

"Just keep your chin up Megan. We'll get through it. I'm sorry for being shouty."

"It's okay. Just go to bed. Night."

"Night. I love you."

"Love you too."

23

We didn't speak for two days after that call.

The day we did, I was walking home from work to see a text from Megan blurred through the raindrops on my screen.

I hope you're well. Thinking of you a lot.

I thought about ignoring it. I had several other messages she'd sent over the last 48 hours, mainly just generic morning texts and goodnights.

I couldn't bear to have another draining argument over nothing, and I knew the mood I was in would make it inevitable. Then again, maybe things had calmed down.

I'll call you when I'm home.

* * *

I took the long way back and got absolutely soaked, but it was worth the time I had to myself. A chance to breathe.

"Jesus. You fall in a lake or something?" Aaron said as I stood in the living room doorway, wet footprints trailing behind me to the front door.

"Here. I'll go get you a towel."

Amy got up and went to their bathroom across the hallway.

"Thanks, Amy. Yeah, turns out it's raining." Amy returned and placed the towel over my head like a shawl.

"There you go, Grandma." She gave me a wry smile and a slight nod as she returned to Aaron's arms.

"No coco either for an old dear like me?" My old lady impression wasn't the best, but we laughed. It felt good to have a little bubble of love. Funny how everything that matters can be completely absent. Even if just for a second. I dried off, wished the love birds goodnight, and went up to bed to call Megan.

"Hey."

"Hey." She sounded sad.

"You okay?"

"Yeah. Not bad. And you?"

"Yeah, good."

What was this? Our voices were monotone. This didn't sound like us. Where was the love and compassion? I sure as hell didn't feel it. Come on,

Lucas. Be better.

"Sorry. I've just got off work and thought I'd take a little time to myself the last few days. How have you really been? Talk to me about it."

"It's okay. You do what you need to do. And er, not great. Struggling quite a bit."

"Anything in particular?"

"Just everything."

"We can talk about it."

"I just don't know who I am or where I fit into everything."

"Maybe you're trying too hard. Maybe you've just gotta let yourself be."

"Well, that's kind of what I wanted to talk to you about." My heart fluttered. Was she breaking up with me?

"I managed to talk to Lisa and get some time off. She was actually really understanding about it, which was a surprise. I thought she would be really pushy with getting me to stay on, but she almost respected it."

"Well, maybe she's not so much of a slave driver after all. I'm glad you have some time off though. I think that's a really good idea. Just having a break from everything and finding some head space. When have you booked it for?"

"I'm going to finish this week, and then from Saturday I'll have a week off. I'm going to go to my parent's house."

"Oh, in France? That's awesome!"

"Yeah..." she trailed off, clearly unfinished.

"Yeah...?"

"I was wondering if you wanted to come and stay?"

I took a moment to think. A chance to get away with Megan and spend some quality time together? A chance to breathe and relax in a place where Megan would be comfortable and feel at home. An escape from London for a couple of days? Maybe this is the opportunity we've been waiting for. And it would be at her house, so no angry farmers. Just a completely safe space.

Somewhere Megan could call home.

"You don't have to come for the whole time. I thought I'd have a few days with myself, and my parents will be home over the weekend too, but they work in Paris, so will leave Tuesday and come back Friday. I think I'll spend some time with them, and then we can have the house. Just me and you until they get back."

"That sounds really nice. Having the space and the time to settle in with your parents and yourself would be really lovely."

"You don't have to... You don't sound too excited about it."

I didn't feel excited about it either. Realistically, I was completely torn. One part of me wanted to go more than anything and was already vividly daydreaming of the times we would spend together.

Going for walks in the mountains. Playing with her dog. Cooking together. Playing video games. Having sex on the sofa. Another part of me hated the idea, and I could actively feel that part trying to scurry away.

My inner monologue went something like this:

Let her have time to herself. You're just going to argue the whole time. Let her go. You can have time to yourself here. How can I be excited after how things have been? Man, this conversation is dragging. I just want to go to bed. Two conflicting narratives raging all-out war in my mind.

Is this what it's like growing up? Just constant internal conflict, never really defining what you want or who you are. Admittedly, I just wanted to go to bed and not think about it. I wanted to go to bed and not wake up again. I shuddered at the thought and felt a hot tingle rush through my body. My palms were starting to sweat, my heart pounded.

"Lucas?"

"Yeah. Sorry. Was just wondering if I could get the time off work. It should be fine. Just give me the dates that you want me. I can get tickets."

"Do you want to come Tuesday night?"

"Sounds good. I'll sort it out now." We stayed on the phone and put a movie on our laptops. I saw no movie, only the dark peeling ceiling as I had done many nights before, the only light coming from my dim phone screen. On the other side, Megan eventually slept.

I leaned over and muted my phone to ensure I wouldn't wake her up and crept downstairs. I made a cup of tea and sat with my elbows on the counter, looking out over the street. It looked like it was a full moon tonight. The lights on the road and apartments started to flicker on.

"Holy shit man, what are you doing sitting here in the dark? You made me jump. I thought you were some Paranormal Activity demon or some shit." Aaron said, hand on his heart. He was wearing Amy's purple fluffy dressing gown and matching slippers.

"Sorry dude. I didn't even realise. I didn't want to turn the light on and wake you up."

"No problem. You okay? No offence, but you look like shit."

"Feel like shit to be honest."

"Bad day?" I thought about it for a moment. Bad day? Bad days had become bad months and, in turn, become bad years.

"Something like that. Want a tea?" Aaron nodded and sat down at the table. "To be fair, can I ask you something?"

"Sure man."

I lowered my voice. "You and Amy. How do you do it? You always seem, I don't know, so happy together. I don't think I've ever heard you argue or anything like that. I don't know. When I see you two, I just feel this love that you have for each other... Okay, that sounded weird, but you know what I mean."

"No, no, I get you man. Well, things aren't always perfect, so know that. If you come in and see us cuddling on the sofa seven times a week, then you're going to think it's great, but you don't see the arguments or the shitty passive-aggressive comments we text each other when we're having a bad day."

"Yeah, I get that."

"But, yeah. I really do love her, and I know she loves me. It really does feel like we're our own little tribe."

"I want that. With Megan, but it's just not there. I feel like the whole time we've been together, it's just been one thing after another. She's constantly holding onto this negativity all the time, and I think I've run out of patience with her. I get pissed off with her just getting a text from her. That can't be right surely?"

"I think with Amy and me, it's all about distance. It was all about distance. We've known each other for like seven years now, but we always had space between us. We went to different colleges and different universities. For the first four years we were together, we probably saw each other once every two weeks, a weekend or something. The longest we were apart was a month, maybe, and that was really hard."

"But she's in Scotland. We have more time apart than any other couple I know."

"Tell me if I'm overstepping Lucas, but you still speak all the time, right? Like texting or calling or on the computer. Maybe you're not giving each other space to be your own people. With Amy, we text and stuff, sure, but we hardly speak throughout the day. When I was in uni, I'd go out for nights out and maybe not speak to her all weekend. We did argue a little bit about it, but that's only because we missed each other. Then, when we were actually together, it was amazing. I remember getting the train to go and see her one weekend neither of us was doing anything as a surprise. It was like a movie. I Googled the time for the last train of the day and ran down to the station, and jumped through the doors a minute before it was supposed to leave. And then being with her after like four hours of travelling was just so good."

"That sounds perfect man."

"But I think that's it. Because we gave each other space to be ourselves, now we can be together because we know who we are individually. There's no pressure to try and be anybody but ourselves. Don't forget though, we have been seven years in the making. How long have you and Megan been together now?"

"Coming up to a year. Ten months, something like that."

"Give it time man. You don't need to decide whether to be with her or not. Why rush to make a decision? Just give it all room to breathe. If you're going to stay together and it's going to work, then slow time. You have a whole lifetime. Take a breath, then you'll know what you want to do."

"Thanks man. That actually really helps."

"No problem. I'm going to bed now anyway.

Thanks for the tea. I'll take it with me. Don't stay up all night. Get some sleep man. I'm sure you'll feel better." We smiled and nodded to each other as he went back to bed.

The bedroom door closed, and the piercing silence of the present moment surrounded me. He was right.

I took a deep breath.

24

I landed at the Montpellier-Méditerranée Airport a little after midday the following Tuesday; the same rucksack hooked over my shoulder that I had travelled Europe with nearly five years before.

This was my first adventure abroad since, and I was surprised by how easy it all seemed, which left me wondering why I didn't travel abroad more often. Within seven hours of waking, I was in a new country.

New smells. New people. New atmospheres. New cultures. Reality was sharp with excitement and possibility. I couldn't help but smile as I walked through the terminal and out the main entrance, immediately hit by the cool end-of-summer breeze and greeted by a beautifully cloudless blue sky, complete with beaming sunshine.

Smartphones certainly made travelling easier. After

enjoying the scenes of passing people for a while, within seconds, I had bus times and maps up on my phone, precisely detailing exactly where I needed to go and when.

I took the shuttle bus from the airport into Montpellier, a tram from one random stop on the outskirts of town to the main train station in the city centre, and then had an hour and a half to kill before taking the train to the small rural town of Arles. It was situated on the rural outskirts of this town where Megan's parents had lived for the last ten years.

I text Megan to tell her I'd arrived okay and would be arriving in Arles around five. Then I immediately switched my phone off, stuffed it deep into my bag, and took some time to myself to explore Montpellier. Fuck, I missed that about travelling.

Aimless wandering through streets that had stood for centuries before I was born. Will stand for centuries more after I'm gone. The city was exactly how I imagined a traditional, some might say romantic, version of southern France to be.

It was beautiful, and I could feel such a spark inside me, a spark that was growing with every street walked, every shop window glanced at, and every person's passing face, into a small lick of flame.

Why oh why had I not travelled more over the last few years?

And by more, I guess I meant at all. I sat and had a croissant and coffee in a small cafe off the main square.

It was a little pricey, and I realised from the laminated menus, written in both French and English, that it was probably for tourists. I didn't mind. I was calm. After lunch, I took some photos of the arches on some of the bigger buildings in the main cobblestoned square and then meandered my way to the train station, finding the platform just in time.

The train pulled away from the city and out into rural southern France. A few small villages and towns passed in a blur, as did the city of Nimes, which surprisingly had its own Amphitheatre, according to the travel guide I'd bought on impulse. I vowed then to one day come back and explore the south of France properly and gave myself permission to experience all the beauty this place clearly held.

Using a pen from the ticket counter, I wrote this within the front cover.

The train pulled into Arles in the early evening while the sun was setting, the air still warm and inviting. I walked out of the station and ventured down a side street that led towards the river Rhone. The scene was nothing short of glorious.

To anybody else, especially the people living here, it surely would have been just another day, but to me, experiencing this other country and realising the world isn't such a small place the size of London, it was everything I needed.

A highlight was the orange sunlight bouncing off the crashing waves on the river's shore. Life glistened. I stood leaning against the wall watching the flow of life for twenty minutes before turning my phone back on to text Megan.

I'm here. I'll meet you out the front of the station?

I walked back up the street and read a few of her messages that were starting to come through; mostly just screenshots of her scores in her afternoon Dream games. I didn't feel nervous, not like meeting her in London, but for the first time in my little European expedition, the feeling of tension in my stomach had started to make itself known.

I'm here.

I'm in the blue Mini

Whereabouts are you?

Out front

Can you be a little more detailed?

Errrrrr, if you look at the front, on the right

I found her within a few minutes parked on the road around the side. I could see her scrolling on her phone through the rear window. She hadn't noticed me behind. I took a deep breath. Just be normal.

"Hey!"

"One second." Megan was texting and had yet to look at me. I leaned over to kiss her cheek and she tilted her head to make it easier.

"Sorry, Lisa is texting me asking where a folder is. And done." She slid her phone into a shelf in the centre shelf of the dashboard.

"You okay?"

"Yeah. Good thanks. You?"

"Yeah. My stomach feels weird because I'm not used to driving on this side of the road. I'm scared I'm going to forget."

"Oh my God, please don't drive on the wrong side. I would like to get to yours alive thanks."

"Well, I hope we will too. I'll try not to drive us off the road and end it all. Romeo and Juliet style." Megan laughed and looked at me. I half-smiled and raised my eyebrows. My stomach wasn't feeling any better.

"Sorry, bad joke," she said.

"Ready?"

"Yup. Whose car is this anyway?"

"It's my mum's. I got insured on it for the week. Makes it easier to come to town. Right. Let's see."

Megan pulled out onto the side street and started to follow the SatNav. For someone scared about driving on the wrong side, she drove in her typically reckless way, narrowly missing the wing mirrors of cars parked on either side of the narrow street and not indicating on the roundabouts. I didn't say anything. What would be the point?

Arles remained beautiful both in the city and out. The city borders held fields of what looked like oilseed, and the horizon dotted with farms and windmills. It was like taking a step back in time, and during the time of year, it being perhaps one of the few last days of summer made it all the more special.

The house lay just on the edge of a country lane, as they often do in France, a few kilometres outside the city. It was stunning, as though it was a property copy and pasted out of a designer catalogue. Perhaps the only house I'd ever describe as breathtaking.

Starting from the driveway, the gravel guided us up to the house, which was bordered by a low cream-coloured wall, topped with orange terracotta potted plants on the little square stone pillars, followed by a small gravel path that led to the front door.

I grazed my fingers across the pots. Still warm from day. Like the ones in old romantic Italian movies, the door itself was a light, turquoise blue that opened up on both the left and the right side. These were topped with a gorgeous curving stone archway.

The house itself was two-storey, with blue wooden shutters open around every window that matched the colour of the door. The stunning finishing touch was the ivy and bushes that grew all up the walls and curved around the windows.

"It's from the 18th Century or something like that. My dad loves it because it used to be the house for an olive farm that was in the fields out back. It was basically falling down when we moved here, but my parents renovated it. It was such a hassle because everything had to be done exactly how it was done back then, but it looks so good now."

"It's really beautiful. It's like a dream." I didn't attempt to hide my awe.

Inside the house didn't disappoint. The downstairs was completely tiled, with large stone fireplaces in most rooms and striking wall to wall windows that opened out into the back garden. There was such a classic rustic feel, I couldn't help but gawp at everything, as though opening my eyes wider would allow me to see even more.

Megan gave me a little tour, introduced me to her dog Cookie, a beautiful spaniel who was very excited to meet me, and we ended up sitting on the patio, watching the chickens peck at the grass and flower beds.

"Ah, it feels so much better now I don't have to drive," she said. She had changed into denim shorts and was wearing a pastel crop top. She looked beautiful, as she always did, especially laying back on the sun lounger with the sunlight kissing her skin. I sat on the sun lounger next to her, stroking Cookie, who sat at my feet wanting attention from the new guy. It was so quiet. A far cry from the noisy London streets.

"I'm glad. It's a bit of a paradise here, hey? So this is where you grew up?"

"Kinda. My dad got a new job when I was like five, and looking to move closer, he found this place. It was run down completely, so it was super cheap. It took a few years to renovate, so we had some trips out here most summers, and then it was done a few years later. The stables I spent most of my time are all over there. Do you want to see them?"

"Sure. Come on, Cookie, you coming with us?" Cookie looked up at me eagerly. Funny. He probably had no idea what I was saying, but the higher-pitched tone of my voice clearly told him that something was about to happen. Dogs made me laugh like that.

He padded alternate paws into the ground with excitement and then suddenly burst off towards the back garden hedge the moment we both stood up. Perhaps he knew already.

The garden spanned the width of the back of the house but was incredibly long, although it wasn't necessarily thin. It must have stretched on several hundred metres, and a tall conifer hedge two or three metres high bordered the outside.

Both sides of the garden had flower beds running the entire length, and there was a line of assorted trees running down the middle spaced several metres apart from one another. Even the trees were beautiful.

I didn't know the tree's names, but I noticed the cherry blossom tree at the back. A few days ago, I'd seen it in a selfie of Megan reading underneath the leaves on one of the patio loungers. I hoped we got to do that together at some point.

We reached the end of the garden, which led to an opening in the hedge and the start of a new gravel path. The path ran straight along the side of a paddock and turned sharply to the right, past more trees, leading us between the fence of the field and the hedge itself. At the end were a cluster of premium-looking wooden stables and a barn.

Climbing through the fence posts into the concrete courtyard of the stables, I knew, like most of my time in France so far, that I was taking a step back in time. Yet this trip was far more intimate.

The stables looked fancy, like a much more well-manicured version of a stable than you'd find anywhere else. This was no chipped or pot-holed concrete courtyard, nor was there much mess of any kind. Immaculately kept. The air was fresh, although there hung the slight tinge of wood preserver that burned my nostrils.

"This was where my horse lived," Megan was beaming, leaning on the gate of a stable, rocking her body on her hands. "His name was Shoelace. It might sound a bit sad, but I think he was my best friend growing up."

"That's a cute name. I don't really know much about horses, so I don't really know what to ask. How many hands was he?"

"About 16, but I rode him when he was younger. We had to sell him in the end."

"How come?"

"I just wasn't here enough. When my dad bought the house, we stayed out here in the summer and then me, Lucy, and mum went back to England, because of school and stuff. I rode him every day during the summers, but I felt bad not seeing him the rest of the year."

"Wasn't he friends with the other horses?"

"Kind of. Dad first managed the stables but didn't really get anyone else coming here. He was too focused on the house and his 'project'. It's only when they moved out here completely that he started renting the space. Poor Shoelace spent most of the time by himself. There was a girl who came up to look after him during the weeks which worked on the farm bit over there, but I only met her once."

"Poor Shoelace." Megan toured me around the stables as the sun continued to set.

I saw the bits of the barn where she slept with her horse and the orchard field to the side where she and her sister would chase each other in the breeze.

25

I had never really heard much about Lucy.

She and Megan had never really been close growing up, and Lucy seemed to keep to herself. She never wanted to go to university nor cared much for education. She had wanted to be an artist.

Her Dad disapproved and thought it impossible to make a decent living with such a 'hippy' mindset. She began dating a French guy she met here one summer and had been with him ever since.

"I was hoping to see Lucy while I was here, to be honest," Megan explained as we walked back along the edge of the field to the house, grazing the top of the tall grass with her fingertips.

"She only lives in the town nearby, but I don't know how well she gets on with mum and dad anymore."

"Haven't you spoken to her?"

"Not really. I took her phone number out of my Dad's phone the day I got here. We text a little, but mum and Dad just avoided the topic when I bought it up. I was going to text her, but I don't really know what to say."

"Well, I'm sure she wouldn't mind seeing you. After all, you are sisters, and you never did anything wrong to her. Parents can just be pushy at times."

"Yeah. We'll see."

We made dinner and watched a movie on the big TV in the fancy living room. Being in this home was like being in a high-class rented cottage for the weekend, and I couldn't believe her parents lived here all the time, nor that this place had basically been her summer house for much of her life. Megan played on her phone most of the night while the movie was on. It pissed me off at first, but I reminded myself it didn't matter.

"I'm so glad I flew here to spend time with you, just to watch you play on your phone, sitting on separate sofas. Great fun," a little voice in my head nagged me to say in multiple variations.

The words varied every time the thought arose, but they all meant the same. All laced with the same notes of bitterness. There was no reason to say anything. What would it achieve?

Megan, however, seemed to pick up on my frustration towards the end of the movie and decided to hop over to my sofa and place her lips on my neck.

It felt nice, but I couldn't shake the bitterness already in my blood. Ah. How I can look back now and see how close I was to taking that night in a different direction.

"What's the matter? Don't you want me to kiss you?" She said, licking my neck a little.

"Sorry. I'm just tired. Not your fault."

"Have I done something wrong?"

"No. Everything's fine." I took a deep breath, trying to reset. I'd love to be in a good mood with Megan right now, I'd love to be in the mood to be together, especially in such a gorgeous setting, but something was holding me back. Megan slumped into the chair.

"Why won't you kiss me back?"

"I'm just not in the mood. Is that okay?"

"I mean, yeah. Sure." We crossed her arms and slouched back. We watched another movie that played after the first. Some fantasy story with castles and dragons and power-hungry queens. I wasn't interested. About halfway through, Megan paused the movie, swung around to face me, and grabbed both of my hands.

"Lucas. Please talk to me. What's wrong?" I took another deep breath before continuing. I couldn't stop it this time. Something erupted.

"I don't know Megan. I don't know how I feel. About us or about myself. Coming here, we're sitting and doing everything that couples do, but there's something in the way. Something I can't quite put my finger on."

"I want to know. You can tell me."

"I guess I just don't know a lot about life right now. When I was in the city, I had a great time. I've had a lot of great times recently, whether that's with friends or my housemates. It's been nice. I have these plans, well, ideas of what I want to do moving forward, but I just feel empty now. It's like all the enthusiasm is gone."

"Lucas. That's horrible. You're saying that's my fault?"

"No, I'm not saying any of it is because of you. I do wish we could talk about it though. I have a lot of horrible thoughts as well, but I don't feel like I can share them with you. I feel like it's such a fine line."

"What sort of things play on your mind?"

"Just us things. A lot. Death things. Plans for the future. Some ideas here and there. It feels like we never talk about any of that stuff. We just play League and talk all the time, but it's never about anything good. I want to feel motivated and inspired.

"Lucas. You can be motivated and inspired. You don't need me or anyone else to do that. You can just do it for yourself. Are you saying I'm, well, us, is holding you back?"

"No. I mean, I don't think so. I just want us to be happy together and then for us to also be our own people. Does that make sense? I think we're both lost and found comfort in each other. Like life is a storm. It's raining really hard, and we just happened to find ourselves under the same tree to shelter from it all."

"Right."

We took a moment to stop and breathe. My senses returned and took stock of the room. Cookie at our feet. The fire crackling. The TV playing softly in the background. A click and a hum of the refrigerator came through from the other room. I broke the silence.

"I think I just need to be around positive energy that's going to inspire me and make life feel good. I think I have a lot of past resentments that I need to let go of. Past resentments with us, I mean. I constantly think about parts of me I hate and I never feel like I can discuss it with you. It's my own shit I need to deal with. I know that. I don't know, I just feel so uneasy."

"I'm sorry you feel like that. I don't want to make you feel like that."

"What about tonight? Just as a recent example. We get here and hang out and go for a walk and that's all fine, and then you just come in, sit down over there, and play on your phone all night. God, it sounds so pathetic saying it aloud, but it makes me feel really sad and bitter. It's horrible. And I can't let it go. I don't want to feel like that anymore. I don't know why I feel like it in the first place. Like, is it right for me to feel like that, or am I overreacting? If I am, what's making me feel like that? Do I just have all these expectations with us? I don't know. Sorry, I know everything I'm saying is so messy. I just can't seem to think straight."

Megan sniffed and gave Cookie a little scratch under the chin. She couldn't seem to look at me, even though it seemed like she was trying to.

"I'm sorry Lucas. I know what you mean. I feel like I'm never thinking straight either. It's just this whole big stream of endless chatter, but at the same time, nothing at all."

"I know. I just wish there was a way we could make it better. I wish there were a way we could help each other. I thought just trying would be enough. You know, just loving each other could make us see things differently."

"I told you, I'm not this cuddly, affectionate person. I wish I was. I wish I could come in and jump on you, cuddle you, and kiss you, but I don't think to do it. I just like having my own space."

"I thought you said with your exes you hated that? You wanted people to be affectionate and nice?"

"I know. You think it's hard? Try being me and having to live with such a contradicting personality."

I could feel my temper rising. I wasn't angry or aggressive. In truth, I just felt lonely. Misunderstood. All I wanted was for Megan to understand what I was saying. I craved it.

"I still don't feel like you understand me. I feel all this frustration inside me. It's like nothing of what I'm saying is getting through."

"How am I not?" Her voice was getting quieter.

"I'm just so fucking torn all the time. It feels like

we're arguing all the time or giving each other space to breathe and think. I'm constantly paranoid that the one time we have space, you're going to freak out and go and sleep with Matt again or something like that. Something has to change."

"I wouldn't. I told you it was a mistake."

"I know. I'm sorry. I just keep thinking about it."

"Maybe I'm just not who you want me to be. Have you ever thought of that? That maybe you're having all these thoughts because I'm not the girl you should be spending your life with?" This slammed the breaks on my racing mind. Emotion settled like the splash of a lake after a large thrown stone had sunk to the bottom.

"What do you mean?"

"I mean that you want this snuggly, cuddly, affectionate person who will jump on you, kiss you in the mornings, and give you cuddles and understand you, but I'm not that person. I wish I was, but I'm not. I can't force it. I just want to be myself and be happy about being myself too, you know? I can't even look after myself, let alone meet all your needs."

"I'm not saying that's all I want. No. It's more about being understood and being positive about life. Having some kind of hope or dream for the future. Not just focusing on all the shit parts all the time. I want to feel inspired and motivated to do something. To be someone. The cuddly nice stuff just fits around that, you know? Of course, I want you to be happy and yourself too. I just don't know why we can't seem to get it right."

It sounded so unrealistic saying it out loud. Was it all just a fantasy I was trying to live for? Was it possible? Was I actually crazy?

Maybe Megan was right. Maybe we just weren't meant to be. Again, hindsight is a wonderful thing. I look back now to those conversations and realise how poorly I was communicating how I felt. How I didn't even understand what I was trying to say, yet still unloading. Lost in it all. No idea what was going on. I had no idea who I was.

"Megan." I took back her hands that had unnoticeably slipped away from mine. Fuck. These words only sounded as fucked up as they did once they had already left my mouth. The mind of a young, hurting person. I'm coming to learn that it doesn't matter who you are, being in a world of pain and resentment and trying to live a life from there is never a sane place to be. Escapes feel limited.

"I don't know. Maybe I'm just forcing something that isn't there. I just truly believed that we were going to be this, god this sounds tragic, this power couple. Christ. I guess we're not on the same page though. Fuck, probably not even in the same book."

"I want to be, Lucas. I desperately want to be. You don't think I wish I was enough for you? You don't think I'd want to do all those things you want to see you smile and to make you happy? Of course I fucking do, but I can't. I'm just going to keep making you miserable. Do you know how much this makes me resent myself?"

Damn.

"I get that we're both in a stage of our lives where we're growing, and changing, and trying to figure out who the fuck we are, but I guess we need to decide whether this is something we can do together or whether it's something we have to do by ourselves." "Lucas. I really love you, and I just want you to be happy."

"I want you to be happy too Megan. More than anything. Do you think we're holding each other back?" Silence hung in the air for an uncomfortable minute. Unaware of the tone of the conversation, Cookie was taking it in turns to lick mine and Megan's toes. I blew air out of my nose when it tickled and looked to Megan only to see her staring into nothingness.

"Megan?"

"Hmm?"

"I want you to be happy. I want you to grow. I want you to turn into the biggest, most beautiful and most wonderful version of yourself possible. I just want to let it all go and start again."

"I don't know what you want from me."

"I just want you to be you and for me to be me. Maybe we could just have a nice few days here, we'll go back home, and we'll have some time just to figure things out and see what that actually means for both of us. We can actually properly figure out what we want out of our lives right now. I think we're putting too much pressure on ourselves. And on us."

Megan looked up at me, locked eyes, and tears started streaming down her face. When she opened her mouth, her voice cracked. It pulled on my heart to see her sitting there and breaking down in such a way.

"I can't Lucas. I can't hurt you anymore. For months, I've just looked at you, and all I can see in your eyes is hate and bitterness. You said it yourself. I can see you're hurting, and it's all my fault. You were so nice to me and I've ruined you. You just said you're a positive person and you want to be happy and I keep pulling you down."

Megan. Please. That's not true. No one is to blame. We're both broken people just trying to find our way and figure out who we are. We can take things one step at a time, and whatever happens, happens. We've just got to do what we can to keep moving forward."

"I'm sorry."

Megan could hardly speak; she was breathing so fast. Was this a panic attack? Her blank eyes were hollow.

"I can't hurt you anymore Lucas. I can't be who you want me to be." "I don't want you to be anyone. Please. Listen to me." I reached out and tried to pull her into my arms, but she sat so rigidly and refused to move.

"Megan, just calm down and listen to me. We're

only talking. It's fine. We'll figure this out, okay?" Without warning, Megan let out a wail, the most horrific sob I had ever heard that seemed to echo around the halls of the house.

Cookie looked at Megan with the most enormous eyes and then looked at me before moving forward slowly to see if everything was okay, placing his head on her leg. I tried one last time to pull Megan into my arms.

She stood up, and before I had a chance to blink, Megan had fled the room. Her bare feet slapped on the tiled floor, and the room then filled with soft thumps as she went upstairs and closed her bedroom door. Okay, I thought to myself. The lounge was oddly still. She's just having a panic attack. I decided to give her a few minutes to calm down and then go check. I petted Cookie a bit.

He looked just as worried as I felt and kept looking towards the door, waiting for her to return. Deep breaths. These conversations were so painful, but they had to happen. Things needed to be said if we both wanted to be happy. The eerie silence of the room continued and it was nothing short of soul-crushing. The walls were closing in fast. I couldn't focus on anything for too long. The furniture. The paused TV. The carpets. Everything was blurred and out of focus. My head felt light. Could I be passing out?

It took a few minutes for everything to feel like it was back to normal. A pressure released in my forehead, and felt as though I was able to think straight for the first time in forever. The room had clarity once again. Cookie was once again lying in front of the TV on the carpet. Apart from the hum of some heating or appliance somewhere behind me, the house was utterly silent.

I listened harder. There was nothing.

I slowly padded barefoot out of the living room and into the hallway to the large wooden staircase that ran up the middle of the house. I tiptoed each step, listening out for any signs that would show where Megan was. I knew her room was the first door on the right, but I had yet to see it for myself.

The upstairs hallway was dark, only lit by the faint glow of the downstairs lights bouncing off the walls. Her bedroom door was closed shut.

"Megan?" I called out, pressing my ear to the door. "Are you okay in there? Can I come in?"

Nothing.

"I'm coming in Megan. I'm sorry about everything. Let's just relax, yeah?"

I pushed open the heavy oak door and found another darkened room. The only light, faint as it was, came from another door on the left. The en-suite.

"Megan?" I called out again. Tiptoeing through her room, I peered into the en-suite, and my stomach dropped.

I instantly began to choke. Unable to breathe. My knees buckled weak, about to collapse under my own weight. Megan was lying in the bath, no water, just a stream of blood pouring from her open wrist that hung over the side. In her other hand was the broken shell plastic razor blade. The blade's metal glinted in the light.

Her eyes were closed.

Her skin white. She didn't move.

26

"MEGAN!"

I rushed over to the bath but had zero idea of what to do. There was so much blood. More blood than I would ever have imagined. I took the razor and placed it gently on the floor, then placed my hands on both sides of her face and peeled open her eyelids slowly with my thumbs. Her eyes were only white; pupils rolled back into her skull. A slight sound escaped her lips.

"Megan, please. What have you done? Fuck."

I was shouting when instinct took over. Megan's phone was sitting on the counter by the sink. The screen lit up with one touch. There was a message from Matthew, waiting just on the home screen.

It registered but meant nothing right now. I tapped the emergency button in the bottom right corner of the lock screen and put the call straight onto speaker.

"Quel service avez-vous besoin?" the operator immediately answered the phone.

"English. English please."

"Service?"

"Ambulance. Please. Send one right now."

"Medical. Your address?" Fuck.

"I don't know. A farm outside of Arles. Wait. I'll run outside."

"How many people?"

"Just one. A girl. She's cut her wrist. She's bleeding and I think she's unconscious." I bolted down the stairs as we spoke and out into the driveway, frantically looking for a sign in the darkness. Just a house name or number. Please fucking God. Literally show me a sign.

"The address please?"

"I don't fucking know. It's a friend's house. I can... Wait." I ran throughout the kitchen and noticed a small pile of letters stacked on the counter next to the fridge.

"Sir?"

"Yes. Yes. I'm in a house on D33. Fontvieille. I will stand on the road with my phone torch on and you can see me. This is the address."

"Yes. Medical is leaving and will be ten minutes. How is the girl?" I leapt three steps at a time, crashing into the bedroom door, and I spun the corner. Megan had sunk down into the bath. The pain of seeing her ripped something inside me. I touched her forehead with my hand. She was ice cold.

"She's not good. Please. Get here faster."

"Few minutes. Stand near road. Safe." I ran back to the road, my fingers covered in sweat, trying to flick on the flashlight. It was pitch black outside, especially with the torchlight beaming. I looked both ways. There was nothing.

"Please," I begged the operator. Desperation laced my voice.

"Where are they?"

"Coming. Stay calm." Blue lights flickered on the horizon.

"They're here."

"Thank you. They will take over now."

The call ended. What happened next I only remember as a blur with only a few moments of clarity.

The flash of the ambulance lights as I directed them into the driveway. Running up the stairs followed by three paramedics. Sitting on the edge of Megan's bed, praying with open eyes that she was going to be okay. French words were answered with the passing of equipment and the beeping of sensors.

Reality blurred again. I was downstairs, locking Cookie in the back room, filling his bowl with food and stroking his head, telling him everything would be okay and he would only be in here for a few hours.

The next, I was in the back of the ambulance.

Megan was wired up to machines and a breathing mask, but still no movement. The paramedics spoke in soft, gentle French. One injected her with something. Another wrote notes. Her clothes were soaked with blood, staining the white tissue paper sheets she lay on.

One of the paramedics spoke to me in broken English, but nothing said was registered. The wave of riding reality in such a way finally crashed in the hospital. I thanked the paramedics as they left once a doctor had arrived with two nurses, locked in a whispered conversation. I sat in the corner in silence, still praying to the universe that everything would be okay.

Nurses came and went. Blood samples were taken, a clipboard passed around. I was asked several questions. Had she taken drugs or alcohol, for example. Finally, a doctor looked over and smiled.

"You are Megan's partner?"

The doctor looked like the image of 'doctor' you'd find next to the dictionary definition. Combed brown hair and thin-rimmed black glasses. His accent was thick, and his face said he was entirely at ease.

"Yes."

"Okay. Sorry for my English, so tell me if you understand."

"Okay."

"Megan is fine. There is a lot of blood. I know. Scary. But she is okay. We think she is faint when she see blood. Many people do this. So sad. They see blood and think they will die. It scares them. She will not die. She is very tired. No major damage. Her body just shocked."

"Oh, that's good. Thank you." Relief swept through me and I felt as though I could breathe once again for the first time. Like the last hour had been spent holding my breath. I felt tension flood out from my feet.

"Yes. She is fine. We can keep her for a few hours. You know? We keep eye on her, make sure everything fine. No infection. And then you can go home. You come in ambulance, so we call taxi. But we wait first. Yes?"

"Yes. Thank you so much."

"The nurse will clean the wound and bandage and then we wait. Okay?"

"Sounds perfect. Thank you so much for your help."

"No problem. I will be over there and nurses can help with anything. Maybe you get some food? Cafeteria is down hall."

"Thank you." The doctor smiled and left. The nurse followed and pulled the curtain. I pulled my seat closer to Megan and placed her hand in mine. There were no words. I sat there, holding her hand and watching her breath calmly.

Someone cried out on the other side of the ward. In my heart, there was nothing but love and compassion. I just wanted the ability to click my fingers for everything to be okay. To go back just an hour and make it all okay. Stop being so bitter and resentful. Love Megan like I was supposed to.

An hour passed and the nurses came and did their thing, leaving Megan again once her arm had been disinfected, had stitches put in, and then been bandaged up. Megan hadn't moved nor said anything to anyone for some reason, though she was awake. It was this absence of being that was still playing on my mind. I waited a few more minutes before leaving our little area to find the doctor.

"Hello? Hey?" I tried to see if I was interrupting. He spun around on his seat and smiled that reassuring smile of his. That dictionary definition smile.

"Hello."

"Hey. I was wondering if the girl in that bit over there was sedated? She's not waking up?" I wish I knew French.

"Anaesthesia?" His accent was strong, but he knew what I was saying. I felt stupid.

"Yes. Why is she asleep?"

"Well, she is probably awake, but we give her injection to make her calm and to slow her heart. She has a little shock. But she is a sad girl. She has lots of sadness inside her and sometimes the sadness can be so much that it makes people not want to move. When she goes home, she will need to see a doctor. Have the therapy. You see?"

"Yes. I understand. Thank you. Sorry for interrupting."

"No problem." He smiled again and returned to the computer screen. I told myself Megan would be fine and decided to walk to the cafeteria to see some new walls. Give myself some time to process. I bought a cup of tea in a squeaky polystyrene cup in the queue and sat at a table in the corner. It was about 11pm at this point, and the seating area was quiet, the lights dimmed.

An older man sat alone a few tables down. Another guy came in through the same door I did, his little boy holding his hand. The child couldn't have been older than four or five and was skipping, a teddy bear in his other hand. His father sat him down at a table and went to the food bar. His expression was bleak.

It was a struggle to stay in the room. My mind kept flicking back to the scene in the bathroom. Her lifeless face. Her sheet-white skin. The way blood dripped down the side of the bath. The sharpness of the razor in her hand.

I replayed it over and over again. My imagination filled in the blanks for what the minutes before I came in must have looked liked. Crying on her bed. Running into the bathroom.

Grabbing the razor and snapping off the plastic casing. Straight into the bath with tears rolling down her face. The cut. Her mind raced that she'd gone too far. The adrenaline. Fear that this might be the way her life ended.

Maybe she was convinced those were her final

moments. I put my head in my hands and tapped my pockets, more out of habit than anything else, to check my keys and my phone. I would have loved to have my phone. I could have just sat and watched mindless videos and waited for everything to blow over. I could have waited for my feelings to disappear. All I had was Megan's phone.

My brain whirred, and then my brain clicked. Matthew's message. I took the phone out of my jean pocket and placed it on the table. I pressed the home key, and there it was.

There was no message preview. I had never looked through someone's phone before and already felt guilty before having already opened it. I had to. I couldn't not. I had seen Megan unlock her phone hundreds of times. 1601. Her birthday.

I tapped the messages app and began to read.

27

Hey. How are you? I've been thinking about you. It's been a while.

I read the message over and over again, several times, each time sparking a new emotion within me. First anger. Then hate. Then pity. Then nothing.

You don't need to ghost me. I was just checking in.

That was the last message sent.

The first sent just five or ten minutes before that. That must have been while we were talking or watching the movie. I scrolled up with one flick but forced myself not to read any of the messages beforehand. It seemed Matthew had been texting perhaps once a week, but Megan had ignored every single message.

The last time she responded she had told Matthew to leave her alone, but this was months ago, just after they had slept together. I closed the app. I couldn't bring myself to look anymore.

What would be the point? What would it achieve?

All that mattered now was making sure Megan was okay and safe. Now and from herself in the future. But what was the plan? What was supposed to happen now?

I tried to sip the already-cold tea in the plastic cup but couldn't stomach it. How was I supposed to get back to Megan's? Maybe I should call someone. Her parents, maybe? God, I couldn't even imagine having that conversation. I haven't even met them, let alone having our first conversation consist of telling them their daughter has hospitalised herself. Maybe there was someone else. Lucy?

The roof light above me flickered and went out with an electric fizzle. I watched the bulb's coil glow fade and disappeared entirely, leaving me in a darkened corner of the room.

The old man looked over from several tables away, up to the light, and nodded toward me with a half-smile. The father didn't notice. He was facing forward, staring into nothingness, lost in his own head. His boy played cheerfully, running a small toy car back and forth across the table. Is ignorance bliss?

I unlocked the phone again and scrolled down

Megan's text messages. The third entry, the last message sent two days ago, was Lucy. I began to overthink what I was going to say, so I just hit the call button and held my breath. The phone rang four times.

"Hey, Megan, what's up?" Lucy didn't sound tired.

"Hey. This isn't Megan. It's Lucas. Megan's…"

"Ah, you're Megan's boyfriend? Heard lots about you. What's the emergency?" Her voice did have a tint of panic.

"Er, yeah. I'm at the hospital at the moment. We came in an hour or so ago. Megan had a bit of a situation. She's okay. There's nothing to worry about."

"Shit. Sorry. What happened?"

"She kinda cut herself." I winced as I said it out loud but still hushed enough so the other tables wouldn't hear. "It's not bad or anything. They've bandaged her up, and she's a bit shaken up and in shock, but she's okay. Sleeping in the ward right now."

"Fuck. I'm glad she's okay. Sorry, I don't really know what to say. Wasn't expecting this call?. You doing okay?"

"Yeah, just a bit surprised, you know?"

"Yeah, of course. Which hospital are you in?"

"Erm, good question. One second." I walked out of the cafe and down the corridor the opposite way I had come, looking for a sign or label somewhere. I eventually noticed it in the top corner of a directional noticeboard. It was a lot harder in French, even though

I should really be able to tell from the typography what the hospital's name was.

"I think it's Hospital D'Arles Hospital Joseph Imbert? Sorry if I'm saying that wrong."

"No, that's right. It's just the other side of town from me. I'll drive over now. I'll be about twenty minutes?"

"That's great. See you soon. Thank you Lucy. It really means a lot. Just go into the emergency bit, and ask for Megan. We're in under her name."

"Thanks. Catch up properly in a bit. I'll leave now."

Click. Back to silence. I waited.

It seemed as though I was checking the time every two minutes, but every gap felt like twenty. I slowly got up, left my cup by the side of the bins where others were stacked, and walked back to the ward. The hospital seemed deserted aside from the odd nurse or doctor crossing the corridor ahead or the ping of a distant elevator finding its floor. Eerie was an understatement.

I crossed the ward and through the double doors to the reception. I stole a glance over to Megan's area through the gap in the curtain. I could see a nurse standing next to the bed, but not Megan herself. I walked on through to the reception as a girl was coming through the automatic doors of the main entrance.

It was unmistakable Lucy. She and Megan had practically identical features, but Lucy had less of a babyface. She had longer hair and looked more mature.

She was a few years older than Megan, perhaps 30, and had various-coloured paints dried onto her hands and arms. However, she must have changed clothes before coming out since they were spotless. The waiting room only had a handful of people sitting around in silence. I caught Lucy's eye and smiled.

"Lucas?"

"Yeah, Lucy?"

"Nice to meet you."

"Yeah. You too. Kinda shitty it was like this."

She breathed a deep sigh.

"How you doing?"

"Yeah. I'm not too bad, thanks. All things considered. Don't think it's really hit, you know?"

"Don't worry. This isn't the first time she's done it. She gets like it sometimes. She's okay still?"

"Yeah. She seems okay. Doctors said she's just in a bit of shock but no real damage. Just some stitches and a bandage. Thanks for coming though, I really didn't know what to do or where to go, being in France and all."

"It's all good. Let's go see her. Lead the way?"

I held the door open for Lucy and nodded in the direction of Megan's bed. Lucy went ahead, peeling back the curtain, the nurse now gone.

"Hey sis. How you doing?" Lucy peered round and stepped into the room that was curtained all the way around. I followed behind.

Megan was awake now, sat upright, and looked startled to see her sister standing in front of her. She looked at Lucy, then to me, then back to Lucy. Then she broke down. The silence of the ward cracked with her cries, tears streaming down her face as her face fell into her hands. Her palms muffled her sobs. My heart ached for her. What could I possibly say?

"Oh, come here sweetie. It's going to be okay. You're okay."

Lucy went straight to sitting on the edge of the bed, wrapped her arms around Megan, and began to pet her hair after Megan collapsed into her lap. I perched on the other side of the bed, rubbed Megan's back, but something didn't feel right. We sat for a minute, Lucy saying little calming things in a low whisper, Megan occasionally trembling with a quiet sob.

"Here. I'll let you guys have some sister time. I'll wait in the cafe bit."

"Yeah. Okay. I'll come and find you," Lucy said.

She then mouthed 'sorry' and gave her best half-smile. Bless Lucy. She was completely on top of it. I shook Megan's phone in the air to show Lucy I still had it and left, closing the curtain behind me.

My mind had calmed down a lot over the last hour or so but was still replaying snippets of the night. The blood running down the side of the bath. Cookie trying to run outside. Waving the ambulance down from the road. The doctor talking about Megan's demons.

What were we supposed to do now?

It must have been our argument that triggered it, and maybe the message from Matthew was the last straw. Compassion reigned. It must be so difficult to deal with it all. I took a deep breath and pushed down the repeating urge to reread the messages.

My hand squeezed the phone tightly in my pocket. There's no denying that Megan needs help. There's no way I can convince her. Hell, there's no way anyone can convince her. It has to come from her. All change has to come from within. Fuck, we could both do with some help. I felt the edges of an epiphany or a lesson coming on, but I pushed it down. There's no time for that right now.

I foolishly told myself that Megan being okay was all that mattered right now, and moving into the future should be an after-thought.

All I can do is be there for her and try to support her as much as possible. No more arguing. No more being selfish. Work on letting go of the bitterness and resentment. Just put Megan first, being there for her when she needs me. Helping her fight her demons and get through to the next bright chapter of her life. I'd been so caught up with my thoughts I hadn't noticed where my walk had taken me.

I'd instinctively left the hospital to get some air but continued to walk down the road. I'd snapped back to reality to find myself walking down a long road only inhabited by street lights and a roundabout at the end.

I didn't realise the hospital was so out of the way of the town.

I followed the road in the cool, quiet night for a few minutes, bounded straight across the roundabout for no apparent reason, and into the outskirts of the main town area. A line of shops stood on the other side of the road. A closed burger bar. A laundrette. Tabac.

It was five minutes from closing. I paid no attention to the shop or the guy behind the narrow counter. Everything felt so blurred. Almost like a daydream or an out-of-body experience, as though I was present for everything, but it felt like somebody else's life. I bought a pack of whatever cigarettes the man gave me. He didn't speak English.

I crossed back over the road to a small wall and sat there smoking. The taste was harsh and coarse on my throat. It had been a while since I'd last smoked, and French cigarettes seemed rougher. Maybe just the brand. I didn't care.

My thoughts paused, and I just sat in the dark of the night, feeling empty and alone.

28

Lucy's name lit up Megan's phone screen half hour later.

I was still sitting on the wall when the vibration of the call knocked me out of my reverie of nothingness and back into reality, like the snapping of a shoelace.

"Hey. How is she?"

"She's okay. One second. Sorry, I was just moving outside. Yeah, she's okay. Just a bit shaky and sad. She managed to smile a little bit though, so I think she's okay."

"Yeah. Well, I'm glad to hear that. I'm outside at the moment. Somewhere down the road. I'll start walking back up."

"Sounds good. Erm, listen Lucas. Megan's feeling a bit fragile, and I think she doesn't want to see you. Shit. That came out wrong. Not that she doesn't want to see you. I think she's a bit guilty and feeling a lot of shame about it all and feels bad about it all happening."

Something crumbled a little inside me.

"No, it's fine. I thought that was the case. Have you got the house address? I'll book a taxi or something."

"Don't worry about that. Meet me outside the front in half an hour, or send me a text when you're here, and I'll give you a lift. They said Megan's fine to stay here a little longer. Then I'll come to see what she wants to do. Can come to mum and dad's, or mine. We'll play it by ear."

"Oh. Thank you. Yeah, that sounds good."

It was gone midnight by the time I reached the front of the hospital entrance, and Lucy was waiting outside, doing something on her phone. I could see her from the road and dropped the half-finished pack of cigarettes in a bin as I crossed the empty car park.

"Hey", she said.

"Hey. We had a little chat. I think she just needs to sleep in her own bed., or at least to get out of the hospital. Ready to go?"

"Already? Can't I see her?"

Lucy paused, locked her phone, and put it in her jacket pocket. She sighed. There was a note of sadness in her expression.

"I don't know Lucas. Maybe go stay at ours, and she'll stay at mine. It's not that she doesn't want to see you. She does. She's just really confused, a bit in shock and a bit upset. Don't take it personally. She just needs a bit of time. Let the dust settle, you know?"

"I mean, yeah. Sure. I get it." I forced a smile and turned to walk towards the car park. I was ready to go.

"I get that it's hard. Come on, let's go get some tea or something and talk it out for a bit." We drove through the night, down empty roads and blurred street lights. We didn't speak. The radio crackled in the background, perhaps a single volume notch up from zero. My body was cold. My mind numb. I thought of nothing.

Waves of tiredness and the nagging absence of nicotine pulled at my senses. I shouldn't have chucked the box away.

We arrived at the house. It didn't look as beautiful as it did in the day. The turquoise shutters, as blue as the Mediterranean Sea, now sat still, and the lovely ivy cast a shadow over them. An outdoor light shone as we crunched up the gravel of the driveway, the beams throwing dark silhouettes of the tree that swayed in the wind all down its length. The dark shapes look like evil spirits dancing on the walls. Demons were here.

"Shit. I didn't pick a key up," I realised as we walked up the path, patting my pockets out of habit. Lucy took the lead.

"No worries. I always keep a spare. I don't know if mum and dad know I have this, but hey. Coming in handy."

The key clicked in the lock and we were greeted

with the sound of Cookie scratching and whimpering at the kitchen door. I freed him as he instantly jumped up, licked my face, and then bounded over to Lucy. He recognised her.

"Hello, boy. How are you?" Amazing how the presence of dogs can take your mind out of any situation. We settled in, turned on the lights, checked the house for anything missed in the earlier rush. Lucy made tea. I sat opposite Lucy at the kitchen table in silence for a while, Lucy catching up with Cookie.

Eventually, tired of the attention, the dog slumped over to his bed by the wall and slipped over sideways. He yawned and closed his eyes.

"It's not about you, Lucas." Lucy started. She was staring right at me. I couldn't feel anything but tiredness.

"Hmm."

"It's not. Megan got like this before."

"She hasn't said."

"When she started at university, she was feeling so much stress. I was still living with her, and she was dating someone on her course. He ended up breaking up with her and leaving her for another girl. One of her friends, if I remember correctly. She was always the type to jump straight into relationships and give everything she has. It's going to backfire like that sometimes."

"I think I've heard bits and pieces."

"Mum and dad put so much pressure on her to get

into Edinburgh as well, so I think she couldn't change her plans. With her boyfriend leaving and the pressures of everything, she just crumpled. I remember finding her in her bedroom. Same as this." I nodded, then shook my head.

"I don't know what to do Lucy. If being with her is making things worse, we can't carry on like this." I felt a single tear rolling down my face.

"Hey man. It's not you. I mean, it might be you," Lucy laughed, "I don't know what's going on, but the problem isn't yours. You can't save her. We can only ever save ourselves."

We let the words hang in the air. Something, I'm not sure what, clicked in the back of my mind.

"I think I'm just caught up trying to help her and save her from herself."

"And who's saving you?"

"I..."

I didn't know. Something clicked.

After all this time, something was starting to make sense. I was lost. Confused. Driven to save Megan. By fixing her, did some part of me believe I would fix myself and my own suffering?

"You don't have to fix anything Lucas. Sam, my boyfriend, went through something similar when he lost his job. He was emotional about everything for months, and no matter what I tried to do, nothing made him feel better. He had to go and sort himself out before things got better. I think Megan is the same."

"Yeah."

"Lucas. I know I'm Megan's sister, but I want to talk person to person." I nodded. "You need to know if you can be there for her and give her what she needs. She needs love and support, and if you don't take her reactions personally, you won't be too hurt by her pushing you away, then stay with her and help her on her journey. You can't make her better, but you can help her. You can be her rock, but only if you're in the right place where you can be that person for her. If you can't take it or you're not in the right place to help her, give her space to heal. Not to cross any boundaries, but it sounds like you're a bit lost as well. I've been there. I can see it in your eyes. Maybe some space to find yourself would be good."

I took a moment to think.

"Yeah. Thank you. That means a lot. Sorry, my head is just spinning right now. I'm too tired to think of anything now." I said. All I could conceptualise at that moment was a bed and the overwhelming urge to go home. The impulsive thought exploded throughout me over the course of a few seconds and pushed all over thoughts out of my head.

"Lucy. I think I'm going to take a plane home tomorrow. I think you're right. I think some thinking time is needed. For Megan too. If I stay here... can she just stay at yours or here or wherever."

"Yeah, that's fine. Completely understandable. I'll

stay with her and make sure she's okay. If you want to go, I think she'll understand. I think she just needs some time to breathe and process everything."

"Thank you Lucy. You're a good sister. I don't know what I would have done without you."

"Don't mention it." We sorted details of leaving a key out, so we both knew where it was, gave Cookie some water, tidied everything away, and Lucy left to pick Megan up and take her back to her apartment in the town.

The door clicked shut and the house, which had seemed full of talk with another human there, became baron and cold. As though the dark spirits drifted throughout the tiled halls were masked by it. I packed my bag and put all my things in one place together by the door and went upstairs to Megan's room.

The bathroom light was still on, but I couldn't help but look in as I leaned around the door to pull the cord.

The blood had dried on the planked wooden side and down the inside of the white interior. Seeing the red glint in the light made my heart beat so fast. I swallowed, cleaned everything up, and switched off the light. I vowed to myself to not go back in there again. I finally lay down in Megan's bed for what felt like the first rest in days.

I had some time to myself, time I had wanted badly. It was far from comfortable alone time, but sleep was soon upon me. Before my eyes shut, I booked a cheap flight for the following afternoon at 2pm back to London and watched YouTube videos of domesticated foxes making weird noises until I couldn't keep my eyes open a moment longer. When my eyes shut, I pictured Megan sitting in what I imagined Lucy's art studio apartment to look like.

She was happy, watching a movie under blankets, giggling and eating popcorn. Lucy's boyfriend came in after Lucy had gone to bed, and he and Megan were kissing on the sofa, cuddling until the early hours of the morning came around.

I thought about texting her, but I wasn't sure what to say.

When I pulled out my phone, I could only see the blurry white fuzz of the electric screen.

29

I took the flight.

A month passed before I saw Megan again.

She stayed in France with her sister for an extra two weeks, lying to her parents by saying she went home early because she had assignments to work on.

To my knowledge, they never found out what happened that night. We didn't even text until she was already back in Edinburgh.

She wrote;

Hey.

I know we're going to have to talk about everything at some point, I just don't know when. I have so much to say, but at the same time I don't know how to say it. I feel like

you hate me. I hate myself. I'm sorry for everything. I really am. I don't know what's going on, but I think this was a bit of a wake-up call for needing to do something.

Anyway, I really hope you're okay, and I really hope I can see you soon. I miss you so much. I wish you had stayed in France and come to Lucy's. Message me back when you can?

I love you so much.

Life rolled forward in the way it always tends to. Aaron had been in his promotion for several months now and left the flat to move into a new Fulham apartment with Amy.

I took this as my chance to move out and start working on my own life, so I made the move back to my parent's house on the outskirts of Cambridge. I took up a job in a warehouse packing boxes but spent my free time brainstorming ideas on how to work for myself.

There was clearly a lot of money to be made on the internet, so my mind was in the place of starting a blog or trying to drop-ship products from China. It was all new to me, but moving back to my place of birth was a chance for rebirth. At this point, it was all about brainstorming and creating ideas.

Many would find this boring. The joy was in seeing the idea come to life and, when it came to growing a business, the process of becoming profitable. For me, this, the brainstorming stage, was the exciting time. This was where the creativity flowed and anything could happen.

And that was the fact of the matter. Despite everything, I felt excited. While it was a bit of a change of pace not having the freedom I had living in my own place, there was no denying it was nice to be home with my parents. I still had to pay a bit of rent, but it was a fraction of London prices, and far nicer to be living in the countryside again.

The long daily walks around the fields and woods in the area were far more refreshing than traversing the sweaty, loud crowds of the city. I frequently wondered why I had ever stayed in London for so long. I only moved there because Aaron wanted a flatmate to share rent. It was never my dream.

Not that I regretted it, but now it was my turn to get things in check. Moving back to the countryside felt like the start of a new chapter. I hadn't spoken to my parents much over the last three years, aside from the odd text message on birthdays and the traditional get together at my brother's over Christmas, so it had been nice to catch up and reconnect.

It was a Friday in November when I sat in my childhood bedroom trying to make a list of possible website ideas. Rain poured, but the sound was muffled out by the sounds of a LoFi playlist softly playing through the desk speaker.

There wasn't much to this kind of music, but it never failed to make me feel relaxed. I was just getting side-tracked by an article titled '4 Ways to Turn Your Man On That Don't Involve Nudity' when my phone fell off the desk with its vibrations.

Megan was on her way down from Edinburgh to stay for the weekend. A few following texts detailed travel plans. Of course, travelling made Megan nervous, especially with the thoughts of whatever conversations were coming up. While I wasn't in the mood for a full-blown conversation right, I did want to make sure she was doing okay. We had plenty of time for everything else when she got here. I glanced at the time.

16:12. She had left just under an hour ago.

The text message lit up my phone for a few seconds before switching off again in the corner of my eye while I finished the third section of the article, wear lingerie around the house, and then switched gears to reply. The text was a single crying emoji.

My heart sunk. I gripped the phone and replied;

What's up?

Someone jumped on the tracks in front. The train's stopped

Oh shit. Are you okay?

* * *

Yeah. I'm not bad, kinda freaking out a bit

Shit. Do you know how long you're going to be sitting there?

Not sure. I'll let you know when I find out.

Okay.

Do you want to call?

No, it's fine. I'll just try keeping myself busy. I'll text you.

Fuck. I wanted to do something to help, but my mind was drawing a blank. I closed the message and switched over to the train app, searching for the Edinburgh to Cambridge line.

At the top of the screen, glaring back, was a big red triangle icon highlighting the problem.

All trains operating on this route will be affected and delayed by an emergency incident. All updates will be posted here and on Twitter. If you are affected by this situation, do not hesitate to call the Mental Health Helpline here.

I sighed. Poor guy or girl.

My imagination showed me several versions of what could have happened and what it may have looked like. Such a horrible thing to do, and the demons that person must have been facing. There must be so much for other people to do, too. Police investigations. Cleanup.

I tried to imagine having to do such a job and flinched at the details. There truly are some hardened people in the world. Or maybe just people who are stronger than I am.

It was a minimum of several hours till Megan got here, that's if she got here by night at all. I left the desk in favour of my bed, perched on the edge, and moved the clothes folded neatly waiting to be my outfit for the evening.

The train was supposed to get into Cambridge at 10 pm with two changes, one in York and one in Peterborough, but there was only a five-minute stop-over between the latter. If she was delayed for hours, it was impossible to make. Maybe she would have to stay in York, get a hotel, and then get a train in the morning?

Fuck.

I sent a single love heart. I could picture Megan freaking out. She came online as soon as my text was delivered. The blue ticks flashed up. Then, she disappeared again. It's fine, I tried to convince myself. She just needs a little time to breathe. Locking the phone and chucking it on the bed, I went downstairs to make a drink.

The last month had been tough. While most days had been spent distracting myself with new ideas and busy with moving, reconnecting with parents and old friends, and working, there was always an underlying feeling it felt I was running from something.

It was always there, I just never shined light on it. The feeling was the absence of love. After France, I'd felt haunted and responsible. I loved Megan, and there was nothing in the world I wanted more than for her to be okay and for us to be happy together.

Every day I woke up and pictured us in our bubble. Walking through London the day we met. Cuddling in bed together. Sitting in the shower at the cottage. Reading to her in the tent by the beautiful summer lake. Walking through the stables in France and hanging out on the patio.

I used to think the year we spent together was full of these beautiful moments, but I slowly realised that they were few and far between.

Had I been deluding myself? Was reality not the same as what I held in my memory? Had I jettisoned all the many bad parts and just kept the shining gems I'd found in the dirt?

We had text little over the last month. I never solidly replied to her long initial text, simply saying we could talk about it all in person. Instead, we sent random messages here and there, never fully engaging in conversation, always replying hours or even days apart.

Over the last week, we decided to put everything aside and start afresh. Just me and her. She would come to the house, stay, and we could try again just to have some us time.

A chance to reconnect and turn a new page. An opportunity to finally spend some quality time together. We were going to put the shit behind us and just concentrate on being us. A month of space had passed and now was our time to move forward. Back in the bubble as we belonged.

She booked her train tickets just five days prior, but as the days ticked by, the more I started to feel that this was probably the last weekend we were ever going to see each other.

I don't know if she thought the same, but neither of us had said anything aloud, despite it being a thought that crossed my mind daily. Our silence on the matter just added pressure. Pressure that fuelled a horrible internal conflict.

I sensed we both felt it. This could be our last chance. Half of me was sad that this whole relationship had perhaps come to its end. Obviously.

Megan was a girl I was head over heels for. I felt a love that had only grown in a strange way each and every day. She was someone who completely changed the way I looked at the world.

A girl who made me want to strive to be a better me. But the other half of me? That was the side of me that knew the end had to happen at some point. We were both broken people living in a broken time of our lives. We may have found refuge from the storm with each other, but now was the time to step back out into the world. It was time to walk on.

Doesn't that mean we deserve one last time together?

Didn't we deserve to put effort into making our last memories together happy ones?

Maybe the fact we hadn't seen each other in so long, especially the last time being in France, that being in each other's arms again would bring back all the feelings of love that felt so distant right now.

30

Hot flushes rippled through me as I stood in the kitchen.

The urge to text Megan again was strong, but I knew I'd be sending it to make myself feel better. I kept repeating to myself that you're not even the one sitting on the train. She said she would text you later. She'll text you when she's ready. You don't need to try and fix anything. Relax.

She text half an hour later.

They say we're going to be setting off in around three hours but could be earlier.

Man, that's so long. How are you holding up? Is everyone on the train okay?

* * *

Yeah, I'm not bad. People are pretty pissed off they're not going places but yeah, just sitting here trying to keep my mind busy.

That's good. Have you got people around you?

Yeah, I'm sitting on my own though

Maybe go speak to someone? Might be distracting.

Maybe. They said they'd organise transport, but I'm not sure if it will take me to yours.

Are you going to find out?

Yeah, maybe in a bit.

Okay. Do you want me to read you a story? I can call and you can just listen?

Yeah... I mean... No, it's okay. I'll do some uni work or something

Okay, well, remember I'm only a text or phone call away Xx

I sighed. The sinking feeling in my stomach was

making me sick. The empty kind of sick. I could tell Megan was trying to make her messages seem as though she was okay, but it was impossible she'd be taking the situation well. I knew her way too well for that. These were all tell-tale signs she was trying to stay grounded but struggling to do so. It was driving me insane.

The image of her in the bathtub, arm hanging over the side, seared across my mind. I forced a deep breath. I saw tears streaming down her face. What could I do about any of it? I had spent some time searching online for things I could say that I hadn't said before to try and get her through the rough times.

Maybe I could share a fantasy of us being together and all the beautiful things we could do together. But did I have fantasies like that anymore? I searched but came up with nothing I thought would work. Goddamn Lucas, stop trying to fix things. She needs to be able to deal with this on her own. No pressure. Just support her if she needs it.

Besides, best-case scenario right now, three hours from now, she'll be on her way here, and it will all be in the past.

Remember, three hours from now, you'll be on your way here. We can cuddle and relax. I've put fresh sheets on the bed and made the room all nice. Do you want to get anything to eat?

* * *

240

I felt useless.

The evening plan was to meet Megan at the train station, but first, I would sneak across the road to the supermarket. A shopping list formed of chocolates, snacks like crisps and dip, sun-dried tomatoes, and maybe even some fake rose petals to spread over the bed.

If they sold fairy lights and flowers, that could be an added bonus. I'd spent all afternoon desperately reading online articles to inspire me to host the best possible date night.

In my mind's eye, I saw the classic movies where a female lead opens the door after getting home from work, completely unsuspecting, to find her home has been set up beautifully.

Shocked by a pleasant surprise, she's forced to sigh, and the moment feels absolutely perfect. Just like the moment she stepped out of the bathroom at the cottage, although I didn't enjoy replaying that memory. That's what I was aiming for anyway. It was a flawless plan.

Megan would definitely have gone to shower as soon as we got home, giving me all the time needed to set everything all up. Now the plans were ruined. Not only would the shop be closed if I was to meet her in town in the early hours of the morning, but she wasn't exactly going to be in the mood for anything romantic.

I had a few hours to kill and thought I should probably go to the gym. It would be good for me, especially now. Although only being home a few weeks, I'd already been getting lazy. The restaurant job had been boring as hell but standing on my feet all day and rushing around after customers was great for keeping fit. Now I was sitting down at a desk pretty much all the hours of the day.

It wasn't healthy and I was starting to feel the effects. My parents had always been avid gym-goers, making it easy to join in and ride on their motivation. If I went with them tonight, not only could I take my mind off everything, but I would also have the opportunity to go to the supermarket to get supplies before it shuts.

As I gazed at the TV blankly, completely lost in my own reverie, Dad got up off the sofa, turned the TV off and tapped my foot with his hand. I looked up to the overly judging look he always gave, subliminally asking whether I was coming with them.

I'm going to go to the gym, and then the supermarket afterwards. Do you want me to get anything?

Megan replied while I was halfway through a run on the treadmill.

I'm fine thank you.

Maybe something for breakfast?

* * *

Sure.

No problem. I'll see what I can find. I know this must sound pretty annoying now, but are you doing okay?

Yeah. A man from the train line was pretty nice and gave me a bottle of water for free, which made me smile.

Aww, that's really nice. Have you eaten? Will you want anything when you get in?

There's some guy down the carriage kicking off though

Some people can be so selfish

Yup.

I ran for an hour to occupy my mind, or rather emptying it by replacing it with tiredness. It worked. I hurried out of the gym and back into humid changing rooms, inhabited mainly by naked older men, which I found strangely not weird, and hid in a cubicle to text without being disturbed.

What's happening?

We have to wait to get to the station in York, then I might be able to get a taxi or a hotel

＊＊＊

Are you going to pay for a hotel?

The train company will pay for it. I don't know. I'll sort it out. Speak soon. Gonna do some uni work.

Okay cool.

Lucas.

Yeah?

I love you.

The words I had been waiting to hear. I was bitter about the situation. Torn between excitement and on the verge of breaking down.

Every time things seemed good or I was excited for something to happen between Megan and me, something would get in the way and make me reconsider entirely whether it was all worth it or not.

Then she would say those beautiful three words and it would instantly cut through the dark and light a fire in my heart.

Suddenly nothing mattered. Only her.

I love you too. Just imagine, in a few hours, even if it's in the morning, you're going to be here, and I'll be able to wrap my arms around you, and we can just crash in bed together and sleep it all off I would like that.

I'm not going to get to Peterborough until one at least.

Are you going to go to bed?

No, of course not. I'll wait up for you. I'll play some games or something

No. Go to sleep. I'll sneak in

You want me to leave a key out?

Yeah, and I can slip into bed, wrap my arms around you, and fall asleep. I can kiss your back and your head and spoon you

Mmmm, that sounds nice, but you don't know where my room is

I'll figure it out.

You gave me the tour, remember?

Yeah, on a video call, you won't know which door to even get in. I could leave you out a map?

Oo, I like that idea. I could be like a spy sneaking around your house I'll leave it by the back door, in the cat flap or something?

OMG, are you actually going to?

Well, I mean, I could do if you wanted one?

It does sound fun

Aha. Yeah, but you don't know the house, or which stairs creak, or how to open the doors quietly. You'll wake my parents up

I'll be super quiet

I'll wait up and hug you as soon as you get here

If I get here

We'll figure it out. If you can get a taxi though, please do. I miss you so much and can't wait to see you.

I miss you too

31

I pushed off the edge of the pool hard into the water.

I hadn't put my goggles on correctly and felt the lenses slowly fill with water leaking in from around the edges. I mostly ignored it and swam with everything I had, trying to make my muscles hurt to push all forms of thinking out of my mind.

Always overthinking. It didn't seem to be getting any better.

Upon reaching the other end, I put my back up against the wall and laid both arms out along the edges. I tensed, kicking my legs softly to float on the water while trying to bring myself into the present. I watched the other people in and around the pool. Tonight was a quiet night.

There were only two other swimmers and a younger couple lounging on the pool chairs to the side, quietly lost in their own little world, oblivious to me watching them. I imagined what it would be like with Megan here in the pool with me.

How everyone else would disappear. We'd spend the whole time floating around, pulling each other through the water in different directions, kissing under the water jets, and lounging around in the steam room and sauna.

We'd flick water at each other and see who could hold their breath the longest.

We'd race up, down and across the pool and act like whales or dolphins, seeing who was able to make the biggest splash. I thought about her sitting on the train alone, trying to process everything that was happening around her. The surreal peace she must be sitting in.

Putting myself in her position, I quickly found myself plagued with dark thoughts. They crept in rapidly. I took a deep breath and sunk down into the pool, letting out just enough air so I could sit at the bottom without having to hold myself there.

What could I do to make things better? At the other end of the next two days, everything would be different.

In the sauna, a 30-something red-headed estate agent told me in detail about her idea for an erotic mermaid novel. I loved it, especially how distracting her enthusiasm was. Afterwards, I showered and got back in the car. I usually sat in the front seat but switched to the back so I could stare at my phone screen.

Zero messages.

I wrote out several attempted texts but decided not to send them, swapping the soppy words and GIFs for the train live tracker app. I lazily watched the train location icon update every few seconds, highlighting its position as it made its way past Newcastle. I told myself over and over again not to check it as we drove through the centre of town, but then what difference did it really make? I couldn't resist.

I asked for a detour to the supermarket before heading home. The store was quiet and was mainly filled with sleepy staff, wheeled cages full of stock, and empty folded cardboard boxes piled against the sides.

There were a few teenagers at the front queuing to buy cigarettes and alcohol for their nights out on the town, and the overhead store lights were blinding compared to the dimmed atmospheric lights of the sauna and swimming pool. I searched high and low for fake rose petals.

The search was hurried since my parents have always been the questioning type and I felt judged, even with just the thought of having to describe that's what I was looking for. It was a fruitless search.

I tried to brainstorm things Megan liked, but she wasn't really much of a foodie and mainly just ate bits and pieces of whatever her housemate had left in the fridge or meals cooked from mail-order food box services. Couldn't go wrong with chocolate though, so

I also bought a share-sized bar of Galaxy and a Chocolate Orange.

There weren't any fairy lights either, and I regretted not keeping the old ones from my apartment that I had hung in all four corners of the roof above the bed. They used to create such a pleasant ambient glow. One I hadn't been bothered to enjoy in a long time.

As far as I knew, they hung on the same roof. On the way out, I considered joining the teenagers in buying a pack of cigarettes. My parents thought I'd stopped smoking years ago, and since Megan hated the smell, I'd never smoked around her. She would realise instantly that I'd caved, and I couldn't be bothered to have that conversation, nor did I want to make her more upset than she probably already would be.

I hadn't smoked since the day before last, so I left the store without anything much, got back in the car and headed home.

As trees and hedgerows hidden by darkness passed my window, I wondered for most of the journey if this were the time I would actually quit the habit for good.

32

Megan didn't arrive until gone 3 am.

The time sailed quickly since I filled the hours with video games and snacks. Megan's text said she'd arrived in Peterborough and was currently organising a taxi to the house. I'd always heard terrible things about train services and how much of a rip off they were, but all things considered, the fact they were paying for a hotel or taxi seemed like a decent thing to do given what had happened. It did cross my mind to suggest Megan stay in Peterborough and take the train company on their hotel offer. It was early morning and she was clearly exhausted by travel.

The fact some guy had committed suicide and she'd been forced to sit in that atmosphere for the last few hours was most certainly doing her no favours. Maybe just going to sleep and getting an early train was best.

But then I wanted her here. Perhaps that's selfish, but I still said nothing.

For some strange reason, feelings of excitement were rising from deep within me, and all the sad and worried feelings were beginning to fade away, revealing much lighter thoughts of seeing Megan and being able to hold her in my arms again. Maybe this was it.

Maybe this was the time we could address everything we needed to address, and it was time to move forward. Our beautiful new beginning starts here.

Still trying to find ways to kill time, I found myself reading a random book of quotes I rediscovered on my bedside table, casually flicking through the book's pages without taking any of the words in.

Occasionally I stopped to admire the hand-drawn cartoons added to some of the pages. One quote caught my eye:

'Two men looked out of prison bars. One saw mud. The other saw stars'.

I smiled.

My phone beeped. Megan had shared her location the same way she did when we first met in London just over a year ago. I tapped the link and watched the tiny green dot moving out of Peterborough, joining the dual carriageway that made up the ring road and sailed off into the night.

I had been watching the train for hours, and now

another dot. It suddenly occurred to me how much of our relationship Megan had been represented by nothing more than a cluster of pixels on a screen. The last half an hour was the longest half hour of the night. I sat cross-legged on the bed, a position I hated because it hurt after a few seconds, but I convinced myself it was good for improving my flexibility.

I pictured Megan sitting silently in the car, staring at the houses of the dark unknown villages passing by, her head resting on the window while her hand tightly grasped the handle on the side of the door. She must be exhausted after coming up to 12 hours of travelling. I was.

While it felt like an age, I realised suddenly the little dot was passing through the centre of the village. She was less than five minutes away. I crept downstairs and walked out across the moonlit driveway. It was beautiful with an autumn chill in the air. The smell of wet leaves. It was raining, but it wasn't as cold as other recent nights. This I knew from my 2 am cigarette breaks, having snuck outside after everyone else had gone to bed.

On an otherwise empty road, car headlights beamed through the trees by the main road, accompanied by the sound of a slowing engine breaking the silence. The lights spun around, flickering the shadows of tree trucks across the gravel and tarmac, flashing again up the dark lane towards me. As the car pulled up, the driver pressed the overhead light, and there she was.

Here we were.

33

"Thank you", she said, tiredness muddying her words as I opened the door. The driver, a prominent Indian man who didn't even turn to look at her, said nothing. A ripple of feeling for her, but not pity, coursed through me.

The moment the car door closed and began to drive off, Megan wrapped her arms around me, buried her face deep into my neck, and pulled herself close while making little closed-mouthed moans with every squeeze.

I wrapped one arm around her waist, my hand on her back, and used my other hand to stroke her hair. Rain rolled down my face. The wind blew, flicking up strands of Megan's beautiful chocolate brown hair, tangling themselves around my fingers as though every part of her was hugging me back.

I felt bliss.

I felt her warmth still held in her body from the overheated taxi, seeping through the pores of her clothes. And yet, she pulled herself somehow closer still. It had been a long month, hell, it had been a long year, but we were together again. The peaceful feeling I adored so much returned. I savoured every single second.

If only it could always be like this. Please, I begged the world, let Megan be feeling it too. Moments passed, and her legs started to shake. Her body trembled. Her shivers rippled through my arms.

"Hey, come on. Let's go inside. It's raining," I said, looking down at Megan, kissing her on the top of her head. She nodded silently and we separated, walking hand in hand back to the house.

"Parents are asleep", I mouthed, taking special care to close the door and turn the key in the lock as quietly as possible. In true 'trying-to-be-quiet fashion', the click of the bolt sliding sounded explosive.

Megan then lost her balance, slipping off one of her shoes and panic-slammed her hand into the cat bed. Fortunately, the cat was out. We crept up the stairs, across the landing and stepped into my childhood bedroom for what was Megan's first time. It was already a surreal experience to have her standing here.

It looked as though she was trying to take it all in. The posters, the travel maps, and the photos on the bookshelf, but the echoes of anxiety and exhaustion were still physically clear, despite the deep curiosity confessed by her eyes. I dropped her bag next to the door and then smoothed some of the creases off the bed.

"Are you okay?" I said, sitting on the edge of the bed. I was unable to take my eyes off her.

"Yeah, I'm tired. A bit panicky still."

"Understandably. Come here" I ushered her to come and sit next to me. She sat and then immediately, without thinking, we wrapped our arms around each other and fell backwards, pushing ourselves up the bed, so our heads met pillows.

"Hey, it's okay. Everything's okay now." I tried sounding as reassuring as possible.

"Do you not shake like this when you're anxious?"

"Not really. I mean, I feel it but don't actually shake. It's okay though. You're probably just overtired."

She nuzzled into my arms a little deeper and felt a wave of relief consume us. I could feel all the tension and dark thoughts that had plagued me for the last few hours begin to fade away while a comforting sleepy feeling took their place. Just as I thought they would. I smiled. Perhaps too convincingly.

All the anticipation of the last month, all the pressure of everything that had happened, had led up to this moment. The time of being together again. I'm sure we both would have agreed the circumstances weren't the best, but even after everything, every good time and bad time, every moment of longing and resentment, here we were, lying in bed at half three in the morning, wrapped up in one another's arms. It was all I had wanted the entire time. Though perhaps I hadn't known that every single day.

"Do you want me to put anything on? Maybe a nature documentary or some sleep music?" I asked, breaking the silence and seeing if Megan had already fallen asleep.

She was on the edge of unconsciousness and tried to mumble something back. As I got up to turn the TV on, about to face the screen in the direction of the bed, she squeezed me tightly, signalling she didn't want me to move.

We lay there, the desk light casting a warm golden glow over the walls, guarding us against the darkness of the world outside. Megan fell asleep and left me gazing at the wall hanging to the left of the bed, tracing the blue and gold patterns of the stitching with a finger on my free hand.

Maybe Megan and I would be able to catch up for lost time by being in the same dream as each other, I thought as I drifted off to sleep.

34

We woke to a scratching sound at the door not more than four hours later, yet neither of us opened our eyes nor acknowledged that the other was awake. It was the light stirring movements we made that gave it away.

I lay listening to the scratches stop and start, followed by a few 'meows' from my cat, Puddles, while she rolled around outside on the hallway floor, eager to come inside as she did most mornings.

I've always thought Puddles to be a bit of an odd name for a cat, but it was on account of her being from the rescue home who found her in a puddle. My parents had the habit of calling her 'Muddy Puddles' when she'd been outside in the rain, always evident from the stream of little paw prints she left on the stone kitchen tiles.

Puddles continued being needy for a few minutes

before I caved and let her in. I opened the door just a crack as she rubbed her face against the doorframe and slowly made her way inside, stopping to sniff the new, unfamiliar bag on the floor.

After her curiosity was satisfied, she made her way around the outside of the room before hopping onto the bed to begin searching for a place to go to sleep again. She was noticeably shocked to realise there was another person in the bed today, and while she usually lay next to me before drifting off, this morning she sat at the other end of the sheets, unsure whether to come any closer.

"Hey there little one", Megan stirred, holding out her hand for Puddles to sniff. Perhaps Megan moved a little too fast, or maybe it's just that Puddles is a twitchy rescue cat who's startled at the best of times, but she immediately sat bolt upright, jumped off the bed and started hanging around by the door to get let back outside.

I hadn't got back into bed because I saw this coming a mile away and quickly ushered Puddles outside with my foot before returning beneath the sheets myself.

"Good morning little one," I whispered back to Megan, kissing her on the cheek while running my arm under her pillow. As I ran my middle fingertip up her spine, Megan arched, pushing her chest closer to me.

She placed a hand on my chest and started slowly running her fingers over my skin for a few seconds before slowly falling back to sleep. We lay like this for an hour or so, alternating who was awake and who was cuddling who before we were both clearly conscious with no signs of going back to sleep any time soon.

"How are you?" I asked. I didn't like waking up and assuming the worst, all things considered. Shit. The bliss from the night before had disappeared with my dreams. The walking on eggshells feeling was back.

"Yeah, I'm okay thank you. Tired."

"It's only like seven now, so that's like four hours of sleep? Jesus."

"Mmm, I want more" Her head pushed deeper into the pillow.

"Can you sleep?"

"No" Megan sat upright, rested her body weight on her hands and sighed. "No, I'm awake now, I think."

"Are you hungry?"

"A little, but not too bad" She turned to look at me and smiled before looking down, scratching the back of her neck. Her sleeve fell slightly, and I saw the scarring of her cut for the first time. A wave of tension and heat flooded over me. I even felt light-headed for a second before a guiding voice in my head told me I needed to do everything I could to ignore it.

Instead, I focused on the fact she definitely still felt anxious. The scratching and vacant stare into nothingness were tells I could always rely on.

Perhaps we could talk it out and go through it all.

Give her a platform to let it out. Try to understand how she was feeling. No. Remember what Lucy said. She'd told me this was Megan's problem to fix. She was right.

Obviously I could be here and support Megan as much as possible, and if she wanted to talk, she would, but I should just focus on being me and doing my best. Why am I always like this? If there were ever a problem in past relationships, I would always try to be the fixer. The diplomatic one. The one offering advice. Obviously it's easy to give advice when you're not at ground zero in any given situation. Talk everything out and leave it in the open to dry.

Megan would rather things were swept under the rug and forgotten about. At least until the pressure built up enough and all the problems exploded out, essentially destroying the rug and ending up with her in hospital. Lucas, stop. This wasn't healthy thinking.

How could I be different? How could I be better?

Maybe just trying to appreciate Megan and make the most of the limited time we had. Time which was now several hours shorter than we had originally intended. It wasn't even that much, but there was such a deep feeling that we had been robbed of precious time. Such a scarce resource. What could I say?

Something along the lines of how everything was going to be alright or about how I was here for her. Some feeling trapped the sentences in my throat. I sighed, pushed all the thinking out of my head, and decided to make this the most peaceful experience I possibly could. It doesn't have to be positive. Just accepting and still. What else is there to do? In any situation, to be fair.

"How about," I said, watching her glancing at her phone while playing with a nail, "we go downstairs, I'll make us some breakfast and then we can go for a walk? Maybe use some energy and go back to sleep?"

"Yeah, that sounds nice" Megan stretched her arms up into the air, the duvet falling to reveal her breasts. I couldn't help but steal a glance, and then I moved forward to kiss her skin from just above her belly button. Moving slowly up her chest and between her breasts, kissing every few centimetres, I only stopped moving up once I'd reached her lips. Her skin was still warm from sleep.

Megan quickly kissed me once on the lips and turned away, swinging herself out of bed, keeping the inside of her arm out of view. I watched her go through her bag, taking out clothes and organising them into small piles on the floor next to her. The deeper into the bag she dove, the more the piles spread across the space between the door and the bed. Everything was okay. The only reason I felt bad was because, so far, this visit hadn't met my expectations.

Damn expectations.

In my fairy tale vision of the weekend, I'd met her the second she was off the train and we'd run into each other's arms, kissing the moment we first touched.

Maybe I would have even picked her up slightly and spun around once while we were still on the platform. I know it's all a bit cliché, but the idea made me smile. It still does now.

"Is it okay if I have a shower first?" she asked, pulling out her wash bag and bottles of hair products, which bought an uncommon yet welcomed fragrance into the room.

"Of course, it's the door just on the other side of the hall." She picked up some of her things and left, leaving both the bedroom and bathroom door slightly ajar so I could see in. I watched her play with her face in the mirror when a sudden realisation hit me. Of course, she was probably feeling dirty and grimy from the train and taxi, so it's no wonder she didn't want to kiss properly.

We hadn't even brushed our teeth before sleeping. I held my hand in front of my mouth and forced an exhale, trying to catch the breath in my nostrils. I didn't smell anything too bad. Maybe a little? How does this even work anyway? I repeated the action several times just to make sure. Still nothing.

"Do you have a towel I can use?" she called out.

"Yeah, let me just get you one." I went out into the hallway to the airing cupboard, grabbed the nicest towel I could find and ran my fingers through my hair, hoping it would stay a little bit upright. I hated it flat. It made me feel goofy. I stared into Megan's eyes in the mirror, but she looked the other way, trying to get something out of her eye.

"Want me to shower with you?" I asked. She said nothing. Instead, she just climbed into the shower, closing the door behind her, and started experimenting with the foreign controls, looking at the tap before tugging at it and jumping back when the water wasn't the right temperature.

"Just turn the middle part to the left. It will get hotter. The water pressure isn't great though," I said. She yelped as cold water continued to pour out. I jumped up to show her the controls, laying our towels on the floor while she adjusted.

Finally, I tested it with my hand and winced as soon as my skin touched the scorching hot water. She always liked the water to burn. I made my excuses and brushed my teeth while she washed behind me. My eyes kept darting over, seeing the shower in the mirror's reflection, trying to catch a glimpse of her wrist, but the glass had already steamed up.

Perhaps just giving her a bit of space to be her own person was what she needed. Maybe it was what I needed too.

"Okay, I'll meet you downstairs. Do you want a cup of tea?" I said. Megan panicked visibly; I could see it in her eyes. Her lips pursed together as though she was holding back tears.

"Do you want tea?" I repeated.

"Sure."

"Normal, or green or..."

"Just normal is fine"

"Sure." I left. Megan locked the door behind me.

Downstairs, the attempt at conversation with my parents, who were sat at the kitchen table eating breakfast, was half-arsed. I was inevitably silent as they conversed about the latest lottery results and something the Prime Minister had said the day before. They were chirpy, excited to meet Megan properly, and I waited for the kettle to boil with unconsciously gritted teeth, bracing myself for any questions they had.

As steam shot out the top of the kettle, I could hear Megan leaving the shower, the water no longer hitting the plastic tray, and instead the creaking of the wood as she sat on the edge of the cupboard next to the bath. The creaks were familiar. What was she thinking about? Maybe the fact my parents were in the house made her uncomfortable. She would be nervous about meeting them for the first time, especially with everything that had happened and feeling so shaken up.

No one wants to meet their partner's parents while on the verge of a panic attack. Maybe I just needed to be a little more understanding. Feelings of empathy started to rise up within me. About time too. I cocked an ear upwards to listen for any further sounds while I poured tea and chipped in with blunt replies to my parent's small talk questions about what we were doing today. I briefly explained why Megan got here so late, and they agreed it was awful circumstances.

They finished up and said their goodbyes, wishing us both a nice day, leaving to spend the morning in town. Minutes after they had shut the door behind them, the sound of Megan's footsteps coming down the stairs filled the hallway.

Outside, the car doors slammed, and the sounds of the car engine and crunching gravel peaked and faded, leaving the house in a solid silence. I stood facing the counter preparing breakfast, taking this split second in time to breathe. It was a stunning morning, made complete by the ocean blue sky clear of clouds.

My gaze fell on the bird feeder just outside the window. As usual, a whole menagerie of birds grabbed their breakfast, but I couldn't identify one. All I saw was a flurry of flapping wings and noisy hopping blurs sporting all the richest colours from gold and red to yellow and blue. It was beautiful. Megan's bare feet padded on the tiles behind me.

"Ah, you're here. Hungry?" I asked, briefly turning away from the counter to glance at her. I couldn't bring myself to make eye contact.

"Take a seat, we have anything you want. Please excuse the mess," acknowledging Megan noticing the crumb-covered plates and half-finished teas from my parent's breakfast.

"Just sit anywhere. I'll tidy it afterwards. What can I get you?" I was trying to inject as much positivity into my voice as possible without it feeling forced. Trying being the key word.

"Have you got toast?" she asked as she began stacking the used plates and mugs in an empty space on the side beside a small pile of letters, salt and pepper shakers, and a laptop.

"Just toast?"

"Just toast."

"Don't you want anything on it? I can make you a bacon sandwich as well if you like?"

"No, just toast on its own is fine, thank you."

"When was the last time you ate something?"

"I had some gum last night?" I couldn't help but let out a stifled laugh. I heard Megan do the same, yet neither of us seemed ready to meet eyes.

"Har har. Very funny." We fell back into silence, me making toast and cutting it all into four cute triangles. Well, they were attempted cute triangles. The first cut was far too wide of an angle and consequently made the other sections stupidly small. Megan couldn't hide her smile at the shapes as I placed the plate down in front of her.

I sat opposite, and we ate in silence, aside from the odd crunch of toast and the bumping sounds of a small bird attacking its reflection in the window behind me. I sensed Megan looking in my direction, trying to catch my eye.

For reasons unknown, I keep myself distracted by flicking through the letters in the pile of post. In truth, it wasn't because I didn't want to look at her, it was just that my mind kept drifting back to what had happened on her train last night. That poor guy. Or girl. That poor guy's family. Why did he do it? Was it a sign from the universe? A metaphor about this weekend? An omen? The death of our relationship?

Christ, that's a fucked-up thought. And self-centred. But all the same... was this the end of us?

It felt like it could be. These weren't alien feelings, and I'd be lying if I said I hadn't felt this way before. That feeling that you're standing on the edge. More like you were standing on the edge but had already taken that first step. Now you're falling and everything that follows is inevitable. So much so that I was trying to make some other poor person's tragedy fit to the narrative of my own sadness. Woven into my own tale.

Didn't that imply everything?

35

After we finished breakfast, we both cleared the table and agreed to go for a walk.

It was truly a beautiful day, and while a bit cold even for November, it was hard not to smile at the brilliant blue skies and stunningly rich slanted beams of sunlight bursting through the trees of the hedgerows.

We walked across the grass on the side of the house, past the patio out back and through a hole in the hedgerow onto a tree-lined dirt path that was, in reality, the driveway for the house next door. We followed a footpath through the trees up the side towards the farm next door.

It was early morning with nobody around, so we hopped the fence to say hello to the sheep, the pigs and chickens, as well as some very friendly donkeys. I watched, hands in pockets, as Megan seemed to become another person. This was a walk I loved when I was younger, the trees I used to run through as a kid and Megan seemed to channel all the same excitement I used to feel. The excitement I had thought she was full of when we first met.

The donkeys plodded their way over and gently bowed their heads in greeting, standing eagerly waiting to be petted, fed, or both. Megan beamed the biggest smile while stroking their hair, commenting on how soft they were, and individually called them beautiful.

"You are so lovely. So sweet," she said to them both, and one even seemed to reply with a smile. Once the donkeys were bored or realised we weren't there to feed them, they plodded back over to the troughs in their stable and we jumped back over the fence onto the footpath and set off up the side of a neighbouring field, the autumn air crisp and refreshing.

At the end of the field, we passed a small woodland where I used to play as a child. I took Megan by the hand and pulled her into a small opening in the tree line. The stretch of trees was about a mile long and led all the way up to the edge of a second field, connecting to the back of the village churchyard, but was no more than 30 metres across. The leaves and branches were thick, the path untrodden besides odd animal tracks and trails that pushed down the undergrowth.

There was barely any sunlight, and being so late in the year, it could have easily been mistaken for the early evening. The only giveaway of day was the beams of sunlight that managed to sneak through cracks in the canopy. They were a morning kind of bright. The air the kind of autumnal that brings you to life.

I watched Megan's eyes lit up as the part of her I adore came to life as we ended this little hidden escape. A part I only ever saw while in nature. As soon as we came off the path, it was as though the spirit of the forest embodied her. As though it was finding a way to be free and explore itself using her body as a vessel.

She took off, running under the branches of the fallen trees, and swinging herself around the trunks, always smiling as she spun around to face me. With the crunching of leaves underfoot, she resembled dust dancing in beams of daylight through an open window.

She ran further ahead and around a circular animal feeder before leaping back towards me as she approached, roaring like a cute baby animal.

"Tag. You're it", she said with a cheeky smile, tagging me on the arm before darting off into the trees again. I followed in pursuit, dipping and diving between the branches, cracking twigs underfoot. Just as I reached within an arm's length of her, Megan reached out suddenly to a nearby tree, swinging her entire body weight around it, then propelling herself off in the opposite direction.

I slid to a halt to take off after her, not realising she'd disappeared from view. I stopped abruptly to listen intently, mentally crosshairing any sound of breaking branches, but all I could hear were the birds startled by our chaos, now returning to their original positions in the trees as if to watch the outcome of our hunt.

To my left was a dense bracket of Loral bushes, their thick, waxy green leaves creating more shadow underneath than anywhere else in the wood.

I scanned the dense brush for openings, of which there were a few, but the entrances remained still and untouched with no branches swaying. Survival instincts kicked in. I walked further down the tree line and eventually found a larger opening in which a person could squeeze in without disrupting the leaves around the outside. I stepped forward.

"BOO!". Megan launched herself out from the side, both hands on my shoulder. The force of movement sent me buckling to the ground.

"I'm going to eat you now," she laughed, burying her head into my neck, kissing my cheek and licking the side of my face once. She pushed herself up and, while still on top of me, rearranged herself slightly and smiled. Perfection, I thought to myself. Despite running for what could only have been a couple of minutes, we were both extremely short of breath. I could feel Megan's heart beating in my own ribcage.

We smiled again and kissed, laying there for a moment, the soft edges of our bubble forming. I felt complete. Neither of us spoke but instead stared into each other's eyes. She looked beautiful, and I don't even think it would have been possible to look away if I had wanted to.

Staring into her beautiful brown eyes, her hair falling from her head around my face, almost framing her, making me feel as though I was looking into her soul and as though I was seeing her properly for the first time. She was art. A bird squawked, causing the bubble to burst.

Megan climbed off me and stood up, pushing a lock away from her face to behind her ear, then pulling on my hand to help me up. Hand in hand, we walked down the centre of the trees towards the church.

One of the first conversations me and Megan ever had sprung to mind as we walked. It was one of our first video calls as we both lay in bed one night, phones propped up against laptop screens and piles of books next to our beds. The conversation felt like a million years ago, yet at the same time, it could have been last night.

"So, what's your favourite thing to do?" I asked.

"I don't know. I love being outdoors. Just in the trees and in nature."

"What about when it's cold and rainy?"

"Yes. All the time. If it's snowing then go for a walk, obviously. If it rains, then even better."

"You walk in the rain much?"

"Well, a few times. I like it. It's peaceful."

What's your favourite part of nature? If you could choose to do anything."

"Can you have a favourite part? All of it. Dur. No, I don't know. I just love it all. I love to be around trees and animals. I used to be really into photography, so I'd go on hikes all the time."

"What made you stop?"

"I don't know really. It was an ex, Oliver, that got me into it. He does it as his job and has like a hundred thousand followers on Instagram. He taught me loads, and we used to do it together, but I don't do it so much anymore."

"Would you ever pick it up again?"

"Well, I used to enjoy it a lot, but it was kind of something we used to do together, so I don't know if I would do it myself. Too many memories there."

"But if you enjoyed it, surely you can't stop just because it's something you did in the past with someone else. I suppose memories and all that, but I don't think something like that should ever stop you from doing the things you love. Do you still go on the hikes and stuff though, even if you're not taking pictures?"

"Not so much anymore either. I'm always so busy with uni, it's just hard to find the time." "So, from when you did go out and about, what's your favourite place?" Megan had looked away from the screen and thought for a moment before answering.

"I adore Iceland. There's so many mountains and beaches and hills and waterfalls. There's something surreal about it. I would love to go back someday. But yeah, basically anywhere where there are forests and outdoor stuff, I'm there."

"Why didn't you choose to do something outdoors with your career then? I know you kinda have, but I mean something a bit more hands-on?"

"I've done conservation projects before, and they were amazing. I don't know really. I would love to live on a farm." I then rolled onto my back and gazed up at the ceiling, fantasising about the same dream, a dream I hadn't shared with anyone for years but had always romanticised the idea of doing one day.

"That's my dream too," I'd admitted.

"Well, one possibility at least. Somewhere in a forest or at the foot of a mountain. Beautiful views. Land for horses or other animals. Space to grow my own food and beaches nearby. Like a big log cabin." We had sighed in pleasure at the imagination we were sharing. Megan added her own details of an open log fire and hardwood floors.

She soon rolled over too, closed her eyes, a smile on her face bigger than I had ever seen. Content in fantasy. I continued the fantasy in a soft, sleepy voice as we grew more tired. I spoke of lying in front of a fireplace on a large rug, watching snowflakes fall outside the window, settling into warmth after a long hike where we saw deer in the trees with falcons and buzzards soaring overhead.

With each added detail, Megan sighed a little with satisfaction, mumbling under her breath things like, 'that sounds nice". I returned the sounds, and we drifted off to sleep. That was one of my favourite of our video calls.

"I don't like being in graveyards. They freak me out," Megan said, staring at a tall gravestone that looked more like a column than a traditional headstone. Her energy roused from being in nature seemed to have evaporated while in my reverie. In my memories, the churchyard looked exactly like it always had, and probably the same for decades or even centuries before I even existed.

The church was old and grey and the graveyard was scattered with headstones poking out the top of long, uncut grass. It seemed nobody came up here anymore.

"What do you think happens after you die? I think that's it and there's nothing else after it. You just rot in the ground like this." She asked without looking at me.

"Hmm, I agree. I think. I don't know. It would be nice if there were more to it than that."

"Like a heaven or a hell?" "Not really. More like moving onto another kind of existence. I watched a video once where a guy gave this speech saying that existence is like the life of a caterpillar. He said being a human and living as we do is the larva form of existence. Then, when we die, it's like the cocoon stage of living, and when we emerge, we're the butterfly. I think he was on drugs though."

"So what do we do as butterflies?"

"Well, we don't turn into butterflies as we know them. Probably just some kind of consciousness that floats around in space. Maybe we get to exist throughout the whole universe." "That sounds pretty boring," she said. It was hard to let that one go. The whole universe boring. Imagine.

She looked so rigid, walking around the graveyard, hands in pockets, mouth hidden by the collar of her zipped-up coat. Megan was gone, but she was also back. "Not if you have senses that detect other things. It's like a whole different form of existing that our little human brains can't even comprehend."

"Meh. I don't know if I believe it." She wasn't listening. I could feel it.

"I'm not saying I believe it. It's just a theory. It would be cool if there were more to it, something like that."

"I guess."

It suddenly struck me how it was still possible to feel deeply alone even while being in someone else's company.

It had only taken a few minutes to walk around the outside of the church, so we were still at the final stages of catching our breath from running through the woods. We walked out of the churchyard and back onto the footpath to return home. I couldn't help but miss the days when me and Megan had been getting to know each other.

Our talks back then had felt long and unending, like

they had no edges. Like maybe we had no edges. We talked about everything and anything and would share opinions and be open-minded about all kinds of ideas.

We would explore everything together. And yet, the more I thought about it, the more I started to doubt whether it had ever been like that at all. Perhaps my memory was deceiving me. Things do always look more beautiful in hindsight. And I had been enchanted, then, falling for a girl living hundreds of miles away. Lonely and trapped in my own world, she had been a portal to a different world. Megan rarely asked for my opinion and never dove deep with me into weird ideas.

I'd always loved spending time talking about new ideas and concepts, even if they made no sense or had no purpose. It was more an exercise in curiosity that I loved than the ideas themselves. It was like a chance to let my mind be free and just go wherever it wanted.

Until that moment, I had always thought that Megan and I shared that love of mental gymnastics, but her responses had shaken something within me. Like reality dawning on me.

There was a pang of doubt or disbelief like a magician had just whipped the sheet off of his glass box, but the girl that was supposed to have disappeared remained visible inside. Stumped. There was confusion, for sure. Irritation, a little. But looming largest: disappointment.

As we walked, I thought back to our past and

couldn't come up with any satisfying conversation we'd had in that sense. Sure, we had spoken a lot about each other's lives and our history, but there weren't any fantasies or daydreams.

Not for now. Sure there were farmhouse-in-the-mountain kind of dreams, but not, hey, let's go on holiday together. Come to think of it, we didn't even have any solid plans as a couple. No holidays or adventures booked.

No plans to move in together or get a pet. No idea on what the future held. Not even wild stabs at what a future could be if it all went just right. We just existed in a solemn, eternal present. I wanted to let go of Megan's hand but couldn't bring myself to do it. Instead, it just fell out. Her grip was so loose as we passed the tree opening where we had first left the footpath for the trees.

We continued straight ahead, following a low wooden fence that looped around a large field and back to the lane we had started on. We walked up the driveway, back into the house, and straight up to the bedroom to catch up on sleep. Sticking to the plan.

We lay in bed, cuddling and spooning each other without saying a word, taking a quick glance at the clock on the bookshelf, I saw it was still only 11 am. I shut my eyes but wasn't tired.

All I could think about was that everything in the past, all these ideas of beauty I had in my head of what this relationship looked like, all these memories, simply weren't true. They were images in my head that I could have fabricated in my dreams, so where the fuck did that leave me here and now? Where did that leave us?

The final image I had before unconsciousness took me tortured. It was of Megan in the bathtub in the bathroom across the hallway from my bedroom, blood dripping from her arm onto the floor in heavy drops like tears. I know I hadn't made that up.

My mind was not my friend today. It hadn't been for years.

36

I stirred awake, glancing over at the clock on the bookcase to see it had just gone midday.

Megan sighed and rolled over as I pretended to stay asleep.

Maybe she'll stroke my face or kiss me, I thought hopefully, but instead, she remained motionless. There was no denying the distant feeling between us had returned. I could see that with my eyes closed. Megan's fingers scraped the surface of the bedside table as she picked up her phone and her fingers began rhythmically tapping the screen as she scrolled.

Feelings of neglect boiled up again, but I decided I'd had enough of torturing myself. Instead, I decided not to care. I didn't care.

"Whatcha doing?" I asked. She locked her phone and placed it face down on the bedside table, and shuffled herself down the bed.

"Been awake long?"

"About two minutes or so. Just woke up."

"Sleep okay?"

"Yeah, not bad actually, you?"

"Yeah, good. Still sleepy, though," I sighed and buried my head in Megan's side. Impulsively, I kissed her waist and then looked up to see her reaction.

Megan forced a smile and sighed. I took this as she wasn't in a playful mood, so I buried my head back down and pulled the duvet over my head. We lay like this for a minute or two. My mind was blank. Not that I was unsure of what to say, more unsure of whether there was anything to say. Eventually, I came up to breathe and sprung out of bed in my usual bouncy way.

"Fancy anything for lunch?"

"I think I'm still full of breakfast."

"What about some more toast? Plain and simple."

Megan thought for a moment.

"Yeah, maybe"

"Come on then," I said, moving some of Megan's clothes off the floor with the side of my foot, carelessly stacking it all into a pile next to her open bag while I pulled on tracksuit bottoms and a hoodie. Megan didn't get out of bed until I had reached the bottom of the stairs. My parents had returned from town and were having lunch, sitting around the kitchen table in the same seats they always sat.

Megan came down the stairs sleepily. She had clearly been wrapped up in her world, lost in thought, and had not heard my parents talking as she stopped abruptly in the hallway at the sight of them, clearly caught off guard. She then continued walking, trying to act as naturally as possible.

"Hey Megan," I started. "This is my mum and dad, Adam and Martha. Mum and dad, this is Megan."

All three said 'hello' over the top of each other and continued talking while I pulled out a chair for Megan to sit next to my father. I went over to the counter to make food.

"What do you do then, Megan? How's Edinburgh?" Dad asked as my parents finished whatever political debate they had been having. I had already told him before, but he was just asking to be polite.

"I'm at university at the moment, studying law."

"Sounds very professional. Enjoying it?"

"Yeah, it's not bad. Your garden is lovely by the way."

They went on with all the expected small talk as I hoped Megan was comfortable speaking to them. I brought over toast for Megan and a bowl of fruit salad for myself. We all chatted for a bit as I tidied up after eating, and we went back upstairs as my parents left to visit the neighbour's house.

After watching my parents cross the lawn and comically hop through a gap in the fence, we settled back on the bed. I looked back at Megan. It was clear she felt identical to me.

A nothingness sat between us. Uncertainty of what to do next. As much as I would have loved to, there was no chance we were going back to sleep this time. This was the moment we had both been waiting for. The silence was unbearable.

I can never tell if it's just my ears in quiet situations, but true silence is always a high-pitched ringing for me, and I've never thought to ask if anyone else can hear it. Maybe it's tinnitus. Years of loud party music taking their toll.

Either way, the high-pitched ringing was just as uncomfortable as nothing. Even the sounds of the birds and cars passing on the main road outside seemed to have vanished. The world was quiet. We were alone. The thought of touching Megan, of cuddling or kissing her, flickered across my mind.

Could we forget all the things that had happened over the last few months that led us right here to this very moment?

"How did we even get here?" Megan said as though she had been reading my mind. I sighed. That's a no on the forgetting idea.

"I don't know, Megan. I just... I just don't know." I looked at her puzzled, unsure of what else to say. What were we supposed to say? Where was this going to go? I felt tears building up. We both knew.

"How are you feeling? Yesterday must have been a weird day. I don't want to get into all this if you're feeling, you know, overwhelmed."

"I'm fine. Just thinking about everything that's happening here." Megan paused, hesitating over whether she wanted to say what she was thinking. She didn't.

Instead, she said nothing and resorted to staring into her lap. Her fingers gently stroked the part of her jumper that hid her cut. Uncertainty hung in the air like thick fog on an autumn morning. I spoke first.

"Are you sure? I mean, with what you went through, especially with your anxiety... I can tell it's playing on your mind."

"I'm fine. I just don't want this to be the last time I see you."

"What are you talking about? Of course it won't be."

That was the wrong thing to say. Probably a lie. Megan looked at me. I couldn't look at her back. Not properly.

"Won't it?"

"Why would it be?"

"Please don't play games with me."

I took a deep breath before answering.

"I don't know what the fuck is going on. That's the honest answer. I want to be with you. I think I love you or know I do. I don't know. I want us to be together and make us work, but it's also such hard work, and nothing seems to work out."

"Yeah. I don't know why we don't just fit together. I have ideas, but..."

"What ideas?" "I don't know. It's just..."

"Just tell me." I sounded blunt. I felt angry. I suddenly had no enthusiasm to carry on this conversation.

"I think you're in love with the idea of me and not me as a person. You always want me to be this loving, affectionate person, but maybe that's just not who I am. I don't know who I am. I don't think you know who you are either."

"Are you saying you want space to figure it out?"

"I... Maybe. I don't know."

"Megan. After what happened in France, if that kind of thing is happening because of us and what we're going through, then I don't know if I can keep going."

"I'm so sorry about that. I didn't know what to do. Everything just got so much. It's the only way I could think to deal with it," she said, pulling her sleeve down.

"We literally didn't talk for a month, and now we're here? Are you kidding me? I've been so worried and not sure about where we are."

"Have you?"

"Of course I have."

Had I? Had I really? Saying this out loud was the first time I'd heard about it, the first time I'd even thought about it.

"I mean, yeah, the last month has been lonely without you," I said, carefully choosing my words. "I've missed you a lot. I've thought about you every day. I was worried and was hoping you were okay. I don't know. I thought I'd give you some space to be with yourself. Should I have text you to show I cared? You should know I do."

"I don't know. There's no right or wrong."

"I don't know. Fuck. I'm so conflicted all the fucking time. I want us, and I don't want us. I can't decide whether it's right or wrong for us to be together. Is it healthy? I don't know about you, but I'm fucking so miserable most of the time and have been for a long time."

"Yeah, I'm miserable too. Can I be honest? This is something I wrote down in my journal."

"Sure."

"I love you. I love you so fucking much with all my heart, but I hate us." That stung. Her words cut through me like razor blades. I winced, but the honesty was absolute.

"Yeah. I see what you mean. I agree. I don't know whether I can help you and help us or whether we need to be on our own for a bit. Even today, all I've been thinking about is how we should probably have space. We're just not fitting."

Megan had tears in her eyes. I watched one drop roll down her cheek, and then, without warning, I saw Megan for the first time. I saw her in a way I hadn't seen her in months. Perhaps ever. Her face. Her beautiful brown eyes glistened with tears. Her lips tensed together and separated with sadness. The way she scrunched her jumper sleeve in her hand. A little freckle on her left cheek.

Again with the sadness in her eyes. God, the fucking sadness in her eyes. Here she was. A human being. A human being I felt so much for, yet in my presence was overflowing with complete sadness and confusion. The suddenness of the present moment hit me like a punch to the face. Everything was crystal clear. Everything was sharp.

"Do you think I'm fucked up?" Megan asked, breaking the silence.

"You're not fucked up,"

"I'm not? I know I am. I'm a broken mess. I'm sorry for everything. I've broken you. You used to be so happy and positive before we met, and now you're just sad and angry all the time."

"I'm not angry all the time? And I definitely wasn't happy before we met. Where are you getting that from?"

"I feel it. I fucking feel it Lucas. Every time you look at me, All I feel is that you resent me." You fucking resent me." Megan broke down further, sobbing into her hands. I didn't know what to say.

"I... don't resent you. Ah, I don't know. Yes, there's probably some bitterness towards you. I'm sure you feel it towards me as well. We would have to let that go." Megan nodded.

"I don't know. I think back to when we first met in London. I felt amazing. You saw the text I wrote you afterwards. I've never felt like that before."

"So you feel that way about me now?"

"Not right now, no."

"You said you love me."

"And I did then, yes. I do now."

"You love me right now. How you loved me after London?"

I thought for a moment.

"No. I guess not."

"But you've said you loved me recently? You text me saying you loved me yesterday night. You only ever say 'I love you' to someone if you really mean it and feel it. It doesn't matter if the other person doesn't say it back. I only want to hear it when it's really felt inside."

For the first time, Megan sounded angry.

"Yeah. I like that way of looking at it."

"So when was the last time you told me you loved me and actually meant it?" I thought again. I tried to scan over the last year and a half. A period of time scattered with a few good moments but riddled with haunted memories and bitterness. I know I felt it towards us, and there's no doubt she must feel it towards me.

"No. I don't know."

This time, Megan didn't cry. I thought she was about to sob, but she just looked straight ahead. Into nothingness. Yet not in a way that she had before. She stayed quiet and said nothing. I knew I had said 'I love you' several times over the last few months, both via phone and text, but she had bought out the truth. I hadn't felt what I would call true love.

At least not like it was at the beginning, even if that was what I thought it was. Not like I felt after London. I hadn't felt like that in a long time. Both me and Megan were breathing slowly and deeply. Megan held her eyes shut for several seconds.

"I do love you, Megan. I do. I mean, I think I do. I just loved you so much after London. Maybe I'm just holding onto those feelings and hoping that maybe one day I can get back there."

"But that's not how you feel now?"

"No."

"I'm sorry."

"I just hate how we're never in sync. Do you remember the drive up to the cottage? I felt so bubbly and full of life that morning and you were so stressed out. I played with you in the supermarket, and danced in the car, and made the cottage all nice when we got there."

"Lucas. I love that you were like that, but you can't fool me. I know. I felt the bitterness. I was in such a dark place then and didn't have the energy to be the person you wanted me to be. To be the person I want to be. You went to kiss me, didn't you? In the supermarket."

"Yeah."

"I didn't want to. I turned away because you know I don't like that sort of thing in public, and there were people around. The look on your face, everything about you said you hated me after that moment, but you just pretended to be happy and not care. I felt it. I felt as though I wasn't good enough."

"I don't hate you. I've never hated you. Don't be stupid. Yeah, there was a bit of bitterness, but I just let it go."

"Did you really? I think you've had all these resentments building up for months and months. I don't think. I know. I see it. I see it in your eyes, even right now. There's so much hate and I can't deal with it anymore."

Megan sobbed into her hands once again. I felt tears running down my own face. She was in so much pain that I could do nothing about it.

Except set her free.

"I want to support you, Megan. I want to support you on whatever journey you need to take to get better. I want you to support me on mine. I want to be there to support everything you do, and I want to do this together. But I think you're right. I think we're too tainted with how we are right now. The past is too strong."

"You can't support me if you don't love me. You just love me how we were. How you imagine us to be. You love this idea of me you're created in your head and that's not who I am. Not right now. Do you know how it makes me feel to look at you and just see someone who hates me?"

"Okay. I get it Megan. Yes. I think it's an image I've used to push everything down. All the neglected feelings and hurt. You know I still think about you and Matthew every day?"

Megan took a deep inhale and held her breath.

I felt tears swelling again and regretted bringing it up, but I wasn't lying. I rearranged myself on the bed, looked out at the window and watched trees swaying in the wind. Megan looked down at her arm and tried to pull a hair out of it with her fingernails. She then pushed her nail into her skin hard enough to make the pressured area turn red.

"I can't help but torture myself with the images of it. I think about him coming over to your house. I think about you crying and then ending up standing in front of him naked, standing and just looking at each other's bodies. I can clearly see him inside you and you making him cum. I can hear you moaning to him--"

"Please, stop. Why are you bringing this up?"

"I'm sorry. I just can't stop thinking about it. I know it was like nine months ago, but it plays on my mind all the time. Yeah, I don't need to go into it. What I mean is it's an example of how I'm holding onto the past and not being able to let it go. I'm really sorry. I don't mean to bring it up like that."

"It makes me so sick to the very bottom of my stomach that you think about it so vividly."

"I don't know. I guess we've invested so much effort into each other. I know I've put a lot of effort and energy into us, and that side of you, that nature-y fun side. I see that in you. I see it come out every now and then, but I also think I see it all the time. That playful, fun side. You know the first few days in France before I got there, and you sent me the video of you rolling around the garden with Cookie? I've still got that on my phone. Hell, even this morning when we were running around in the trees. You get this look on your face, this smile that I don't see any other time. It's like all the worries have gone out of your head, and you're just happy to be alive."

"That does happen, and I do forget myself. It just doesn't last for very long."

"But if you know that's how you find happiness, why don't you try and focus on that? Why don't you try and bring more of that into your life?"

"You know why."

"Because of your course?"

Megan nodded, then shrugged. I felt like the course was an excuse, but what would telling her help? Nothing at all.

"So, what do we do?"

"We've tried having space before, but we keep ending up back here."

All I could see in Megan's eyes was raw pain, and I couldn't help but wonder if it had always been there. Perhaps I just hadn't looked hard enough to see it. Maybe my fantasies of us had clouded everything I saw. Fuck. I didn't even know what was real anymore.

My mind had betrayed me in so many ways. I felt like a victim of myself.

"Lucas, I love you so much. Like really love you. I want to be with you, but something just isn't right here. I'm so broken, and I don't know how to fix myself. I need to discover who I am and find out what I want in life. I'm not like you, I don't see the positives in everything. I don't see life as this big, amazing, beautiful adventure where you can embrace it and just love every second.

I thought you could pull me up to be with you, but it doesn't work like that. I'm surviving. If you're thriving, I'm just coping. I'm just trying to get through the day from beginning to the end."

"I wish I could help."

"I need to find my own solutions. Walk my own path, as you would say." That would have been funny, and I would have shown it if this was a place to laugh.

"I guess we both have things to deal with and stuff to work on ourselves."

"Yeah. I guess we do."

Without realising, we had zoned out from the rest of the world while talking. We were in a bubble alright, but not the sort either of us wanted to be in. Everything from the bed to the walls to the wind and the trees outside felt surreal, as though they had suddenly been bought into existence, and we were both seeing it all for the first time. I felt trapped and the world felt small.

"Come here," I said, stretching my arms towards Megan. She folded at the hips, still crossed legs, and placed her head in my neck, and tucked her arms into me. We sat like this for a minute before silently agreeing it was uncomfortable.

We broke apart, and I laid down on my back, opening my arm out again for Megan to lay down next to me. Once we settled in, we pulled each other closer and sighed. She kissed the side of my chest.

If only we could freeze time, I knew we could lay in this moment forever.

37

By the time I checked the clock, it was gone five in the evening.

We had spent most of the afternoon watching a series of random movies in near-silence while in each other's arms. The sun was starting to go down.

"Are you getting hungry?" I asked, moving away from Megan and sitting up on the edge of the bed to stretch my legs.

"Sure, I could eat. Are we going to have dinner with your parents?"

I gave her a 'are you serious' look.

"We can wait for them to finish and go down after? They'll be eating until about half six."

"Yeah, I think after. I don't want to be rude, but I don't think I want to sit with them. Especially if I won't see them again."

"Hey, don't say that. We can still talk and maybe see each other again in the future."

"Really?" she asked before shaking her head, then she fixed her eyes on me.

"No Lucas, we can't. We've spoken about this."

"Yeah, but if we're taking the time to work on ourselves, then there's no reason you and I couldn't work out in the future."

"Lucas. Stop. This is going to take time. I don't want the pressure of that. I just want to take things slow and steady and do what I need to do. I don't want to drag you down with me."

I knew what Megan was saying was right. I had my own shit to sort out. She had hers. Yet again, this afternoon, or at least the last few hours, was a prime example of how great everything could be. I didn't want to let go. The possibility of having something so beautiful again fulfilled me in such an unsatisfying way. I wasn't ready to let go, but I understood.

Again, my mind deceived me. A relationship isn't formed on an afternoon of cuddles and kisses. The foundations of love aren't based in affection. It's based on something far more inexplicable.

"I know what you're saying. I'm sorry," I said.

"It's fine. I just know I'm not in a good place. I think I'm going to get worse before things start to get better."

"That terrifies me."

"I'm sorry."

"I just have these images in my head that I don't hear from you for ages, or weeks, or months, and then one day I find out you've killed yourself and that's it."

"I'm not going to kill myself. I'm far away from that point."

"I don't know that though. How can you be sure? France was terrifying, and I'm sure it was for you too. Do you know what it's like to see you get into that depressed state of mind? I'm sorry. I know I sound selfish and it's not about that, it's about you finding reason, or purpose, or meaning. I'm just saying it's scary. I care about you a hell of a lot Megan."

"I care about you a lot too. I have to go through this though. I don't know where I'm going, but I have to get through it."

"I know, and I know you need to make your own mistakes. We both do. I want to love you and support you no matter what, and if that means letting you go to figure things out, then I guess so be it."

"You too. I can't bear the fact I've hurt you so badly. It breaks my heart you've probably got images in your head you're never going to forget. I can tell it's something you think about and feel all the time. I know you've got to get over that, and I don't think it helps messaging each other or waiting for phone calls. It's almost triggering, and you'll never be able to let it go."

"Yeah, triggering is a good word for it. Okay, well, that's decided. Want to play a game or something before we cook? What do you fancy to eat anyway?"

"Mmm, stir fry?"

"Sure, I'll have to see what we've got, but I'm sure I can manage that. Shall we play a game?"

"Yeah, I just need to charge my laptop for a bit."

League. The same game we always played. The game that had brought us to each other. Our escape. We set our laptops up and sat at my desk in the corner of the bedroom, rearranging everything so we could sit comfortably. I put Megan in my normal chair, and then I got another from the office to sit at the end of the table next to her.

As the game loaded and we waited for Megan's laptop to have enough charge, Megan perched herself on my swivel desk chair and stuck out one leg, resting it on the bed behind us. Without thinking, I put a hand on her leg and stroked her with my fingertips. She closed her eyes and leaned back. Neither of us spoke. My parents were talking to each other downstairs, but the conversation could only be heard as a faint mumble through the floor.

"Hey, let me sit where you are," I said, standing up and ushering Megan to get out of the chair. Megan stood up. I slipped in behind her and then nodded for her to sit on my lap. My hands instantly wrapped around her into a perfect cuddle. We fit together, and I was transported back to London.

Those awkward first moments. I guess sometimes it works and sometimes it doesn't. We lent back into the chair as Megan placed her hands around me and squeezed tightly. She turned as much as she could in my arms and we kissed. The cuddle got tighter. We rested our foreheads together, breaking for a moment, only to sign into the game once Megan's computer had loaded.

As Megan copied the Wi-Fi password from my computer, my hands made their way between her thighs. I ran my fingertips up the inside as gently as possible and moved my head into Megan's neck, giving her small soft kisses. I felt her skin instantly prickle and she became hot between her legs, and I could feel her legs tensing on me. I kissed and bit the skin on her neck and shoulder. She moved to make it easier.

After a few kisses, Megan took my hand and pulled me towards her in the direction of the bed, causing the chair to roll across the floor a little until it hit the edge. I rolled out of the chair and up the bed we found each other in each other's arms by the time we reached the pillow. We kissed intensely. We undressed. I started to kiss her neck, making my way down her body until I reached between her legs. The sex was intense.

We snapped back to reality forty minutes later to the sound of my mum gently knocking on the bedroom wall as she walked up the stairs.

"Lucas," she said as she reached the door.

"Is it safe to come in?" This was always how she knocked on the door, and used to when I had a girlfriend over as a teenager. She was always awkward like that.

"I wouldn't if I was you", I called back, still naked under the duvet. Megan stirred sleepily and pulled the sheet up closer, terrified that my mum would open the door. She didn't.

"There's some dinner left in the microwave if you two want some. Just wondering if you were still alive. Have you even been outside today?"

"Yes, we went for a walk earlier. And thank you. I'll have it tomorrow. We're going to make a stir-fry or something soon."

"Okay then," Mum said, and we watched the roof of the room, listening as she made her way back downstairs. Megan and I made dinner quietly, laughing at some comedy show my parents were watching loudly in the other room before heading back upstairs. Everything seemed effortless.

We cut vegetables together and threw carrot peelings at each other. We slurped noodles and flicked each other with tea towels as we dried the plates afterwards. We scurried back up the stairs into my room, and Megan tried to tickle my feet from behind with every step I took. We crashed onto the bed and stuck a random movie on from Netflix.

"What time did you say your train tomorrow was?" I asked. The question hit me in the gut, even though I had asked it.

"About midday."

"You'll need to get a taxi. It's Sunday, so no buses."

"That's okay" "Yeah, I've got a number for a cheap one."

"It doesn't matter."

"Want me to come with you?"

"No, it's okay. You'll only have to come back."

"Okay."

The final bars of sunlight beaming through the windows, just about cutting their way through the trees outside. Within minutes, they were gone. We barely spoke to each other and lay side-by-side on the bed, watching the final minutes of light fade and darkness shroud everything. All we could see was our own reflections in the blackness of the windowpane.

"What's your favourite sport?" Megan asked, "and your favourite subject. Did you enjoy school?"

"That's a lot of questions. Why do you ask?"

"I don't know. I'm just curious. And we're in your childhood room..."

"I'd rather talk about us."

"Please. I want to know."

"Okay, well, I quite liked all lessons, except maybe languages. And yeah, I quite liked going to school. I guess I like learning. I've always thought it's not the lesson you don't like, it's the teacher. If you don't like the teacher, you're never going to like the lesson.

"Yeah, that's true. What sports did you like?"

"I liked all sports. Mainly running and badminton. I was mean at badminton. I used to play for a local team under 16s. It's weird because I used to do sports all the time. I can't remember when I stopped." Megan smiled.

"Can we play badminton one day? I'm not very good, but I think you could teach me?" I paused, glancing over at Megan to see if she was being serious. As far as I could tell, she was. I decided to humour her.

"Sure. Be warned though, I won't hold back. I'll make you run from side to side and then when you won't be able to get it, I'll smash the shuttlecock over."

"That's okay. I like running. And shuttlecock's an amusing word." We both laughed. Strange how there's always a moment to smile during the deepest pain. We looked at each other and, for a split second, there was only us. I looked into her eyes and saw her. I knew that she had seen me.

"You know, you've never told me your favourite lessons," I said, "Did you like school?"

"No. I hated it."

I couldn't figure out why we were going through these topics of conversation. We had already covered them in the 'getting to know you' part of the relationship nearly a year ago. I scrunched up my face and looked over to Megan. She sat up, cross-legged, half on a pillow, her hands in her lap, tightly holding the duvet with white-knuckled fists.

"I hated school," she continued, "I just hate being told what to do. I hated it so much. Teachers told me where to go and where to be. Who I could sit with and who I could talk to. I think I might have also been a drug addict in school."

This I didn't know.

"What? That's a bit random."

"I smoked weed and do bits of coke with the sixth formers during my GCSEs. I mean, not during the tests, but you know."

"Wow, that doesn't sound great. I mean, you were a teenager. I'm not saying I haven't done it, but yeah."

"I was a horrible teenager. I don't think my parents love me. Do I even love them?"

"Megan. Stop. Please."

"I'm sorry. I'm just freaking out a bit."

"You reckon?" We laughed.

"I just – I just don't want to lose you."

"Megan."

"I really love you, Lucas."

"I – I don't know what to say."

"Say nothing." "You know, I think I'm now starting to get it now."

"How so?"

"Well, you're not happy with your life, but that's so understandable. You've been screwed around by boyfriends and pressured by your parents and supervisor. All of it hurts and has left a lot of pain. No one helped you through the hard times and it's all building up. You're so self-destructive and I thought that I could help, but I can't. I can't be a fixer. No one can be a fixer. You can only ever save yourself and hope that you can become a beacon that shows others the way. Never directly. You need to learn how to love yourself before you can love anyone else. I do too. We both found ourselves in a dark place together and thought the other was light. But we have to learn to see that light within ourselves."

"You don't need to fix me Lucas, that's right. But I want you to know you've opened my eyes to so many things. I've never felt as happy as when I've been with you. I'm really sorry. I didn't want to hurt you. I want you to be happy and to support you and you raise you up. I wanted us to raise each other up into something amazing."

"Don't worry. I know I have my own set of problems too, and those held us down. It's not on you. This past year, hell, I've been stuck in such a deep rut the past few years. I thought when you came along, you had chucked me a rope down and were pulling me out. I think it's more accurate to say we bumped into each other in the dark."

"Not so lonely, was it?"

"Where has this Megan been the last five months? Hell, where has this Megan been the last year?"

"I don't know. To be honest, I feel like you're actually seeing me for the first time. I feel seen, if that makes sense? I feel calm too. Peaceful even."

"Me too."

We lay down next to each other on the bed, staring at the ceiling. I played with my own fingers, unsure whether I should reach out and stroke her. Megan was the first to stretch out her finger and stroke the back of my hand. I instantly replied by stroking back, and within seconds we were holding hands and rolling onto our sides to face each other. I slid my arm under the pillow holding Megan's head, and emotional exhaustion pushed her off to sleep without saying another word.

I lay awake for a while, savouring the atmosphere of the room. There was no tension. It felt like there hadn't been a moment of silence here in hours, yet now everything seemed strangely calm and peaceful. The room didn't feel sad.

There were no tears. It was just simple serenity holding us in place. I realised I was clenching and unclenching my jaw, something I always did when I was tired and stressed.

Waves of tiredness and feelings of being drained mentally washed over us.

Within minutes we were both asleep.

38

Megan jolted awake as if from a bad dream, waking me in the process.

I pulled her closer, still pretending to be asleep, but managed to steal a glance at the clock. 10 am.

I treasured having her in my arms and felt as though she was thinking the same thing. We both clung to this moment a little longer. We lay for a bit before Megan slipped out of bed and started packing all her clothes away from where they lay around the room, slipping them quietly into the rucksack she had left open in the corner.

"Are you okay?" I said.

"Yeah, are you?"

"Yeah, I'm not bad."

"How are you feeling about travel?"

"Yeah, no, I'm fine."

"Okay good. Do you want me to book the taxi?"

"Sure." I searched for the taxi number. I called, booking it for an hour's time. I asked how much and checked with Megan if she was happy with it. She agreed, not really listening to any of the questions.

I imagined her imagining the idea of staying here, or what would happen if I took the train with her, or even taking a train somewhere else together. Somewhere new. Could we start a new life together somewhere? I snapped back with the taxi operator confirming the booking.

"It's going to be here in an hour," I said as soon as I hung up the phone.

"Are we still going to be friends?"

"I don't know if that's a good idea."

"I just. I'm sorry. I'm not going to make an arse of myself."

"Don't worry. If you have something to say, now's the time to say it."

"It really doesn't matter anymore, does it?"

"Maybe if we do get better and find ourselves or whatever you want to call it, we could make it work. I don't know. I don't want to put an idea of love in our heads for some far-off future, but you know what I mean. Maybe it's just a case of wrong time, wrong place."

"Perhaps."

The rest of the hour passed slowly, with neither Megan nor me really speaking. We talked briefly about some of my travel photos on the wall and the fact that we hoped the train journey back would be less eventful than the journey here. I apologised several times for Megan taking the train all the way to my parent's house on what was eventually an 18-hour round trip.

She said it was okay and didn't mind. It was nice to have a change of scenery. There was really nothing more to say.

Despite the hour passing slowly, the taxi arrived suddenly and we shared an awkward last moment. Megan picked up the bag she had left by the front door while debating whether or not to go to the toilet before she left, but the taxi pulled into the driveway before she decided.

I held the door open and lent in for a final kiss, mostly out of habit, but Megan had already stepped out onto the driveway. She didn't turn around to look back and instead threw her bag over her shoulder and got into the car, smiling at the driver as she did so. I closed the door and went and sat in the kitchen before the taxi had pulled away.

She was free.

I filled that afternoon with video games and tried to think of anything but Megan, failing miserably to do so. I found myself lost that evening, browsing pictures of our time together. Several times, I picked up my phone and gazed at Megan's online status on various platforms, but she was never there.

The green dot had vanished, always set with a dull grey. An hour after Megan was supposed to have gotten home, I couldn't resist sending a text.

Thank you for coming. Everything aside, it was good to see you. I wish you all the best. You'll always have a place in my heart.

I regretted it instantly and couldn't shake the image of Megan uncontrollably crying on her bed, the text message on her phone screen next to her.

Two weeks later, I received a text back.

There's not a day when I don't think about you.

I don't know if you'll care or not about this, but I want to tell you. I've taken up meditation and I'm getting serious about journaling and it's really helping me learn about myself and my emotions. I'm on my last course of antidepressants, and then I'm trying talk therapy. It made me really sad to see you had unfollowed me on everything, but I guess it's for the best.

Sorry, I don't know why I'm telling you all this. I'm just letting you know that I'm really working on myself. I want to be a better person. I miss you and love you a lot.

I replied two days later.

Hey. I hope you're okay.

I'm glad to hear that you're working on yourself and it sounds like it's really paying off. I'm the same. I feel my happy energy coming back, or at least some kind of negative stuff is fading away. I know it's too early to say anything, but breathing feels good, and I hope you feel the same.

Look after yourself.

About a month later, I looked at Megan's social media profiles for the last time.

Another week passed before I realised that I hadn't even thought about checking it, and I smiled to myself, writing a reminder to celebrate the little wins in my journal.

Two months had passed when I video called Megan accidentally from my pocket.

After apologising several times, I asked how she was doing, and she told me all about work and how she found her talk therapy was really helping her understand and deal with her emotions and gave her a way of letting go of her past. We stayed on the phone for two hours.

Four days later, Megan messaged me saying she enjoyed the video call and wondered if I was about at the weekend for another, just to catch up and see how I was doing. I told her I was busy Saturday but could do Monday night instead. Megan agreed. Saturday came, and I spent the day on a date with a girl I met through a dating app.

Charlotte.

She was lovely and seemed to have a heart of gold. She was teaching herself to knit and bought me a hat she had finished the day before. It was rainbow coloured, and by the end of the day, it was falling apart, but I still wore it the entire time we rowed down the river through the city in a hired canoe. I had fun but missed Megan with all my heart and couldn't stop thinking about the upcoming phone call.

I thanked Charlotte for such a lovely day but told her I was still getting over someone, and I didn't want to hold her back or make things complicated for her.

She said she had a lovely time as well, and she would like to catch up as friends someday. Monday came, and after half an hour of catching up, Megan and I started arguing. During the week, Megan had become really upset and stressed and met up with Matthew. He came over and helped her move some drawers up the stairs to her bedroom.

He had tried it on, but Megan refused his advances and asked him to leave. I didn't know why I felt upset, but all the old feelings I thought were gone were kind of back. Far less intense than the times before, perhaps I was just reminded they had at one point existed. It was nice not to feel resentment. I was moving on slowly. We hung up, agreeing that it was a bad idea to call.

I tried once more, nearly three months after seeing her for the last time, but Megan had blocked my number.

We never spoke again.

39

As I sit in Edinburgh Waverley, I watch a beautiful woman walk towards me through the main terminal from the stairs that lead up to the high street. She's carrying two shopping bags, one in each hand, wearing a semi-formal red business dress, high heels, and the cheeky smile I fell in love with as we made eye contact.

I laugh to myself as a few guys turn their heads in her direction, momentarily fading out their conversations, while she makes her way through the cafe and over to the table. They're forgotten as soon as she places her bags next to me, leans forward, and kisses me on the cheek. I catch her lips with mine mid-kiss.

"Hey. That kiss was for your cheek. That's not fair. You stole it."

"Sorry. Here you go." I tilt my head to show my cheek again.

"No. Tough luck. That was the only one you're allowed." I can't help but smile.

"How are you?"

"Good, thank you, beautiful. How was the city?"

"Good. Got some stunning bits for the house. I'll show you when we get home."

"Can't wait."

"Are you okay, Lucas? You seem a bit distant."

The kids on the sofa opposite left long ago. Instead, there sits a girl with long brunette hair. A starlight-grey hat. She's slim. Tapping away on her laptop.

Could it be? No, surely not. It isn't.

I'm taken back to the tent, and the woods, the lake, the countless video calls, and my bedroom in my parent's house. I see Charlotte in front of me, and the sense of peace is overwhelming.

"Yeah. The last time I was here, I was with Megan and came up to see her. Was just thinking about it all. Seems like so long ago now."

"You're not about to run off and go and find her, are you?" Charlotte's cheeky smile was everything.

"No. Not at all. I mean, the me from back then feels so long ago. Everything felt so intense and emotional all the time. It's like I was striving for love, needing some kind of love so badly that I would do anything to get it. Just the whole time failing to notice that I needed that love from within myself."

"You know," Charlotte leaned forward to a low, faux, seductive whisper, "I love it when you get deep and spiritual with me."

"Har har. Very funny. It's just interesting to think about an old version of me and see how far everything has come and how much everything has grown." I leaned forward and kissed Charlotte sweetly across the table, taking her hand and squeezing it gently, never breaking eye contact.

"And how beautiful everything has become."

Loving Megan was one of the hardest things I'd ever done. It was a constant challenge to figure out how to act and how to be. A battle to find myself and my footing. Did I take too much of her depression so personally? Did I support her in the right way? No one will ever know. Although I'd probably take a guess and say no.

Perhaps I had been lost so deeply in my own struggles that I failed to clearly see what was right and wrong. My eyes, unable to see reality for what it was, were fogged by my own thoughts and feelings. Lost in images and fantasies of what I thought I wanted and what I believed to be true. If I could go back, would I do anything differently?

Of course I would. I could hate myself for the way I acted, so selfishly but out of a place of pain. There is no right or wrong.

Deep down, I know I gave it everything I had and tried my best. I really believed I gave her all the love I had to give, and I did, but I know I didn't have much to give. Maybe I did, leaving none for myself, and so the downhill descent began.

Then again, maybe we were just two human beings running through the woods who got caught out in the rain on the same day. Lost, afraid, and alone, we bumped into each other under the same tree, a shelter from the storm. Under the tree, we held each other close, begging desperately, pleading with the gods for the storm to pass.

We thought we had come to save each other when really we were but a sign that we needed to save ourselves. The only way one can ever appreciate the beauty of the summer days is by living through the darker depths of winter.

As we board the train home, my heart is with Megan.

Not a heart full of romantic love or craving desperate wanting, but one full of friendship and peace. The feelings of one compassionate human to another. I sent my love to her through the universe, wishing that she was okay and had found her way.

Wishing that she had set out to find herself and had been able to love whatever she discovered.

Wishing that she was free.

40

Hey there!

I just want to take a moment to express how grateful I am for you showing interest in this book.

Although simple, this book and its story mean a hell of a lot to me, and while only my debut (and I know it's not perfect), I hope it's the beginning of something beautiful. I also hope you found meaning within these pages or at least kept you entertained for a few hours.

I would absolutely love to hear your thoughts and what this book did to you, good or bad, so if this story moved you in any way or you want to support me, I would be eternally grateful if you left a review wherever you got this book.

It helps me out massively, and I would love to hear your thoughts so I can keep working towards becoming the best writer I can be, whatever that may be. T

Thank you again for giving me your time, and I hope you got something out of it more than anything.

Lots of Love

Mike :)